ENDORSEMENTS

'At a time when atheistic autocracies are increasing at a threatening pace, there is an even greater imperative for Christians to see Christ re-established at the centre of both our culture and our personal lives. Cindy lays out the secret of recovery that makes this book indispensable for any Christian wanting to be on Christ's side of history.'

Jim Wallace AM,
Canberra

'Fifty years on from the Jesus revolution, Cindy McGarvie shows how it is time for a modern-day version of the Jesus Movement to erupt. A movement where modern-day filters are removed, bondages are broken, and people of all ages and from all walks of life find true freedom by giving their allegiance to Jesus Christ. Are we ready?'

Barry Borneman,
Former CEO of Wycliffe Australia

'All kinds of "wokeness", together with new forms of expressive individualism and self-definition, and even the digital metaverse, have brought a slew of new challenges since the first edition of Cindy McGarvie's *#JesusRevolution* in 2018. How quickly things change! This book can help us avoid deception, so it deserves a place on every pastor's bookshelf.'

Phil Campbell,
Senior Minister
The Scots' Church, Melbourne

'Cindy Mcgarvie's book is a resource manual that ensures the reader will be able to trace the *why* of the philosophies and worldviews of writers and thinkers such as Karl Marx and Timothy Leary, who not only experimented with their beliefs but implemented them in government rule (Marx) and lifestyle (Leary). Nothing short of another Jesus revolution that releases a sequence of tsunami waves of love and truth will rescue the nations.'

Peter Brownhill
Director of Youth with a Mission (YWAM), Perth

'Cindy looks at the many different movements, revolutions, and ideologies that have been intentional for decades at shaping culture and society, while it would seem the church has been asleep. With great opposition come great opportunities for the church. This book challenges the body of Christ to rise and respond in practical ways and engage in this life and death battle. *The Next Revolution* will both inform you and stir you to action.'

Letitia Shelton,
Founder of City Women,
Author of *Disruptive Women*

'*The Next Revolution* is not a book for the faint-hearted. McGarvie sends out a clarion call to the next generation to turn from the post-modern cult of self-importance and embrace a renewed understanding of, and commitment to, the beatific vision of the kingdom of God that Christ inaugurated here on the earth.'

Sandra Godde, theologian, lecturer,
Author of *Reaching for Immortality*

The Next Revolution

Resisting the Cult of the Self

CINDY MCGARVIE

YOUTH
FOR AUSTRALIA
CHRIST
PUBLISHING

The Next Revolution: Resisting the Cult of the Self
Copyright © 2022 by Cindy McGarvie

Publisher: YFC Australia, www.yfc.org.au
Youth for Christ Australia is a chartered member nation of Youth for Christ International.

All rights reserved. All Youth for Christ Australia materials, regardless of format, are protected by copyright law. No part may be reproduced and reused for any commercial purpose without written permission from Youth for Christ Australia. For permission requests, write to Youth for Christ Australia via the website or email address info@yfc.org.au.

The author asserts her moral rights.

All Scripture references are from the New American Standard Bible® (NASB), unless otherwise noted. Copyright © 1960, 1962, 1963, 1968, 1971, 1972, 1973, 1975, 1977, 1995 by The Lockman Foundation. Used by permission. www.Lockman.org.

Scripture quotations marked (NKJV) are taken from the New King James Version®. Copyright © 1982 by Thomas Nelson. Used by permission. All rights reserved.

Scripture quotations marked (NIV) are taken from the Holy Bible, New International Version®, NIV®. Copyright ©1973, 1978, 1984, 2011 by Biblica, Inc.™ Used by permission of Zondervan. All rights reserved worldwide. www.zondervan.com.

Many parts of this book were first published in *#JesusRevolution: Real & Radical*, November 2018, by the same author.

Editing and Typesetting: Sally Hanan at Inksnatcher.com
Cover Design: Michael Speelman at representcreative.com.au

ISBN 978-0-6483954-3-0
ISBN eBook 978-0-6483954-4-7

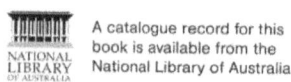
A catalogue record for this book is available from the National Library of Australia

This book is dedicated to the young people today who carry the tremendous calling to lead their generation back to the ancient biblical pathways established by our Creator, God.

CONTENTS

Foreword i
Preface v

1. The Jesus People Revolution 1
    What Billy Graham Said about the Jesus People Movement 5
    The Fire Burns Out 7
    Purity, Selflessness, and Brotherly Love 8

2. Philosophies That Fuelled the Counter-Culture 10
    Philosophies 12
    The Most Influential Philosopher of Our Time 13
    The Russian Bolsheviks Implement Marxist Philosophy 15
    The Long March through the Institutions 18
    The Great Refusal 21
    Expressive Individualism 23
    From Boomers to Gen Z 24

3. The Civil Rights Movement 28
    A Parallel Movement 30
    A New Black Power Movement—Black Lives Matter 33
    The Social Justice Gospel 36

4. The Psychedelic Revolution 40
    LSD: 'Turn On, Tune In, and Drop Out' 41
    Smokin' Weed for Breakfast 43
    Psychedelics and Drugs of the 21st Century 44
    Weapon of Mass Destruction—The Opioid Crisis 47

    A Biblical Response 49

5. The New Psychedelics 55
    Aldous Huxley and His *Brave New World*............................ 56
    The New Psychedelics 58

6. The Spiritual Revolution 62
    Gurus and Pilgrims 63
    Hippies and the Occult 66
    The New Age Movement 68
    The Human Potential Movement 70

7. The Self Movements 76
    The Self-Esteem Movement 76
    The Self-Help Movement... 80

8. New Age Syncretism 85
    The New Thought Movement 86
    Young People and New Thought 88
    Oneness and Other Things... 90
    Perennialism.. 92
    The Pagan Cult of Gaia 94
    The Cult of the Self... 96

9. The Sexual Revolution... 99
    It Started with a Pill 100
    The New Sexual Revolution 106
    The Ideas Driving Today's Sexual Revolution 108
    A Secular Perspective 111

10. The Women's Liberation Movement......................... 116
    The 'Nameless Aching Dissatisfaction' 117
    The Sexual Revolution and Women's Movement Unite........... 119

    Women's Liberation 121

    Reaping the Benefits Today 125

    The Fallout of Feminism's Sexual Freedom Advocacy 128

    A Biblical Perspective 131

11. The Environmental Movement 135

    The '70s Ice Age Scare 136

    From Conservationism to Environmentalism 137

    Real Threats or Not? 140

    Earth Day: Bringing the Environment to the Fore 142

    The Christian Response 143

12. The Antiwar Movement 149

    Antiwar, Flower Power Hippies 151

    Vietnam, the Unpopular War 152

    Vietnam Ends in Unnecessary Defeat 154

    History Repeats 158

    Young Balladeers Step Up to Articulate the Mood 160

    How the Church Responded to the Vietnam War 161

13. Why Young People Hate Capitalism 164

    For a 'Moral and Religious People' 165

    The Demise of Capitalism 166

    The World Economic Forum 168

    Late Capitalism 172

    Artificial Intelligence Provides Hope for Young People 175

    A Biblical Response 176

14. The Family and Church 182

    The God of *Self* 183

    Psychology Usurps the Bible 184

 Discipleship Deficit 187
 The Fastest-Growing Religion 191
 What the Church Must Do to Resist Selfism 193

15. The Me Generation 196
 Increasing Godlessness 197
 The Digital Revolution 198
 The Metaverse 200
 The Loneliness Epidemic 201
 Untethered Orphans 204

16. The Early Church Counter-Culture 207
 Can I Be Called Anything but What I Am? 207
 The Neopaganism of the West 210
 The Inversion of Christianity 213
 Christians in Secular Culture 218
 Persecution of Christians Today 219

17. Christian Resistance 222
 Could Persecution Happen in the West Today? 223
 The Christian Family as a Resistance Cell 226
 The Local Church Fellowship as a Resistance Cell 228
 Suffering Is a Source of Great Strength 231

18. The Next Revolution 234
 Jesus Chose Twelve Young Men 235
 It Started with Prayer 238
 I Want God and I Want Freedom 241

Acknowledgements 244
About the Author 245

FOREWORD

'Of making many books there is no end, and much study wearies the body' (Ecclesiastes 12). There are numerous books seeking to explain what is happening in our wider society. Non-Christian authors like Douglas Murray, Jordan Peterson, and Lionel Shriver are important cultural analysts, but although good at identifying the problems of our culture, they struggle to provide the solution. On the other hand, there are many preachers of the gospel who struggle to connect it to the society and people we seek to reach.

The author of Chronicles tells of the 'men of Issachar who understood the times, and knew what Israel should do' (1 Chronicles 12:32). Jesus rebuked the crowd: 'Hypocrites! You know how to interpret the appearance of the earth and the sky. How is it that you don't know how to interpret this present time?' (Luke 12:56).

In Australia, as in other Western countries, the church is struggling in its search to understand the times. We have swum in cultural waters for so long that we find it difficult to see where everything is going. Such is the pace of change. The people in our society, and often in the church, are confused and lost, like sheep without a shepherd. The temptation for the church is to retreat into its bunkers, lash out, and end up in as much despair and confusion as the rest of the culture. That need not be. We need men and women who understand the times and who can communicate that to our young people.

Which is where Cindy McGarvie comes in. I do not know Cindy, so when I was given this book, I was able to approach it without preconceptions and prejudice and read it with all the usual measure of realistic cynicism that a Scottish Presbyterian in exile could be expected to muster! I was pleasantly surprised.

This is an excellent work, managing to combine cultural analysis with scriptural faithfulness and practical biblical application. Cindy avoids the twin traps of simplistic cliches or giving the impression that without a PhD you cannot understand what is going on.

It is particularly helpful to look at how Cindy lays out the various 'movements' or 'revolutions' that have arisen in Western societies. Although much of the analysis is of what has happened in the US, this is also appropriate for Australia and other Western societies because of the enormous cultural, political, and social influence the US has and continues to have—in progressive chaos theory, a professor catches a cold in Harvard and an earthquake occurs in Sydney!

One of our great difficulties is that the church will often find itself responding to the latest consequence of one of these revolutions but not understand where it is all coming from. If we react, then we just appear to be reactionary. If we stay silent, we appear to acquiesce. It is only when we understand the roots that we can deal with the fruits.

The question arises: if this book is about the culture of the self, then why does it deal with Marxist philosophies, the Civil Rights Movement, the psychedelic revolution, the New Age movement, the sexual revolution, the women's liberation movement, the environmental movement, the anti-war movement, and the anti-capitalism movement? The answer is because all these movements have become tied up in the self of identarian politics. Ideology in the 21st century has become all about 'Me'! The cult of the self colours every ideology. How else can you explain a world in which billionaires can profess themselves as communists, politicians speak of women's rights but can't tell you what a woman is, and teenagers believe the earth is doomed whilst continuing to enjoy all the fruits of the capitalism they blame?

And herein lies the beauty of *The Next Revolution*. It is not a right-wing polemic offering political solutions to deeper problems. Reacting in a worldly way to the world's wrong solutions would not be helpful. The trouble with the movements advancing women's liberation or civil rights or the environment is not that they are completely wrong; it is that they don't go far enough. They are not revolutionary enough. If we just change those in charge of the system, then in the words of the band The Who, we 'meet the new boss, same as the old boss'. If we destroy the system, what do we replace it with? Our middle-class revolutionaries are happy to tear down the family structure on which society has been based for thousands of years, but they don't know what to replace it with.

The world doesn't need a Christianity which goes along with the Zeitgeist or one that retreats from such a messed-up world. What the world needs is the Christianity that turns the world upside down (Acts 17:6). We can only have that if we know Christ and his Word in a deeper sense, and if we know the culture and people we are seeking to reach.

Cindy speaks of the Christian resistance. This is not just 'raging against the machine'. It is rather a counter-culture. A real revolution. Cindy helpfully points out how the Jesus movement revolution ended up fading away. The lesson is not that we don't need another such revolution rather than we need to learn from the past and pray that the next revolution will be deeper and last longer.

My experience has been that young people are the ones who are most likely to find the radical nature of Christ appealing, which is why I would unhesitatingly commend *The Next Revolution*. It is precisely the kind of book that Australian young Christians need, and not just Australia's; this works well in any Western culture. It would also greatly benefit older Christians and non-Christians alike. It is not a shallow dip but rather a deep, quick dive into profound matters.

As you read this book, enjoy, question, think, pray, and act. There may be things you disagree with or would express differently. Good! Iron sharpens iron. Cindy's book is not the answer; Christ alone is, but this book does as good a job as any of pointing to him and demonstrating how we must communicate Christ in a post-Christian world. May the Lord have mercy on us all.

—David Robertson, The ASK Project, Sydney

PREFACE

This book started out as a second edition of my first book, *#JesusRevolution: Real and Radical*, that was published in 2018, hence some similar structure and content. However, as I began writing and researching, I realised that this book had to be different. I continuously saw patterns of major secular philosophical ideas and influences that have infiltrated churches and Christian thinking significantly, to the point that I believe the church has been greatly weakened. The Christian church desperately needs to be able to stand strong and resist the cultural tsunami that is carrying away our young ones. And this is why I decided to change the focus of the book to become an exposé of the strategic onslaught against the Christian faith, so that we are not unaware of the schemes of the enemy.

Over the years, I've been able to read widely about our current culture, and I have shared my thoughts and observations with other Christians, as well as spoken with many young people. Through this, I came to realise that I could help and encourage my Christian brethren by writing about these current challenges that we are facing. I care deeply about the next generation, particularly our boys (hence my previous book *Lost Boys*), and I believe that our young people must be equipped to both discern empty philosophies, intelligently refute them, and steadfastly resist their influence.

I realise that not many people keep up to date with social and political issues, nor do they know history well. In fact, Christians are often accused of extreme ignorance in these matters. In addition, the general level of biblical understanding and literacy of Christians seems to have plummeted, and this puts them at greater risk of absorbing well-sounding ideas that turn their eyes inward to self.

Throughout this book, my intention is to translate to you what I've observed and learned, bringing history, culture, social issues, politics, and faith all into perspective to expose the philosophies and ideas that have crept into churches and Christian thinking since the cultural revolution of the '60s and '70s. With our cultural foundations being dismantled, we are replacing our faith in God with self-worship. It is my hope and prayer that this generation of young people will lead a strong resistance against the cult of the self.

This book is for Christians both young and old, and it's my hope that many young people will read it. No matter your age, if you are struggling to understand the world and the rapid pace of things changing, then this book is for you. May the eyes of your understanding be opened, and may you be inspired to join *the next revolution*.

— 1 —

The Jesus People Revolution

It is little known that John Lennon was a false prophet.

In 1966, a public outcry arose in the West after a newspaper, the *London Evening Standard*, featured an interview with John Lennon who said the Beatles were 'more popular than Jesus'. In fact, what Lennon actually said was, 'Christianity will go. It will vanish and shrink. I needn't argue about that; I know I'm right and I will be proved right. We're more popular than Jesus now. I don't know which will go first—rock & roll or Christianity. Jesus was all right, but his disciples were thick and ordinary. It's them twisting it that ruins it for me.'[1]

Only one year after Lennon's 'prophecy' about the fate of Christianity, a youth revival bubbled to the surface and burst forth, originating with the very demographic that included the Beatles' biggest fans. Within the turmoil of the '60s, hippies began encountering Jesus and were radically converted en masse. This revival was believed to have started in San Francisco amongst the most *lost* and rebellious young people, and it spread like wildfire across the nation. Sparks flew to other nations around the world, including Europe and Australia. The movement lasted around ten years, dying down by the late

1970s. These converted hippies were nicknamed 'Jesus People' or 'Jesus Freaks'.

No one knows the exact details of the revival's origins, but the most publicised and documented time was in San Francisco over the summer break of 1967, referred to as the 'summer of love'. This was college break time, when hippies flocked from all over the nation to a place called Haight-Ashbury, where they enjoyed weeks of free love, drugs, live rock music, and communal living.

Some of the local churches reached out to these hippies to share the gospel.[2] The most effective evangelists were converted hippies who could speak the hippie jive and understand the culture. Some of the *square* young evangelists had challenges in connecting with the hippies and found that it helped to grow out their hair and sideburns and change their clothes to bell-bottom trousers and bright shirts, and to accompany former hippie converts. Churches didn't take too well to this adaptation of appearance, and it created tensions amongst congregations and church leadership.

Tens of thousands of hippies were converted over that first summer and in the following years. In San Francisco Bay, there were mass baptisms. Coffee houses were established around the area by Jesus Freaks—converted hippies—to reach out to those sleeping rough and tripping out on acid. Those making the pilgrimage to the summer of love city were advised to bring a sleeping bag, warm clothes, and money instead of just the flowers in their hair—referring to 'San Francisco', a popular song at the time that encouraged people to wear flowers in their hair and be prepared for a love-in there.[3]

Little did they know that behind the scenes, powerful prayer warriors were praying for revival amongst the young people of their nation, particularly the hippies in San Francisco. Of the prayer groups, some had been meeting for many years. One was a Californian group called the Golden Candlestick, which started in the late thirties to early forties and consisted of a group of ladies committed to lifelong prayer and intercession.[4] (Their powerful prayer ministry has gone unnoticed and unrecognised.) I heard a friend's firsthand account of the times. She was converted during the Jesus People Movement and discipled by Kay Smith, the wife of Pastor Chuck Smith of Calvary Chapel. This church became renowned for mass baptisms of converted hippies in southern California—the ones you see in the typical historical accounts of the Jesus revolution. My friend told me that it was Kay who first encouraged her husband to pray with her for the hippies. It was the result of those prayers that they began to reach out.

An article in *Calvary Chapel* magazine gives some insight to the situation and the challenges they faced:

> "No bare feet allowed," read Pastor Chuck Smith as he approached the church door early one Sunday morning in the late 1960s. Angry and sad, Chuck removed the handwritten sign. Many in the fellowship he had been leading for several years were embracing their pastor's desire to welcome streams of young people—mostly beaded, bearded, and barefooted—regardless of the countercultural individuals' hygiene or lifestyle. But the sign indicated to Chuck that some congregants were focused on preserving the building's brand-new carpet.
>
> At the following church board meeting, Chuck expressed his and his wife Kay's vision to impact the next generation for Christ. "We will love these kids and teach them God's Word," Chuck challenged the leaders of the fellowship, an independent church in Southern California simply called Calvary Chapel. They had already taught the new believers James 2:1–4, he

pointed out: "My brethren, do not hold the faith of our Lord Jesus Christ, the Lord of glory, with partiality. For if there should come into your assembly a man with gold rings, in fine apparel, and there should also come in a poor man in filthy clothes, and you pay attention to the one wearing the fine clothes... have you not shown partiality among yourselves, and become judges with evil thoughts?" How could the church discriminate against the shoeless and shower-less, Chuck asked, after teaching them that Scripture? The point was well taken. From then on, Calvary Chapel's leaders resolved to love the young hippies more than they valued material goods—or their own way of life.[5]

As converted hippies entered mainstream churches, they brought with them a refreshing new approach. They were more relational instead of formal, dressed casually rather than in stiff, Sunday-best clothes. In addition, the Jesus People influence helped churches to connect with youth culture. However, this didn't happen overnight; it took years for some churches to fully embrace change, particularly their music choices. The Jesus Freaks' new music was called Jesus music. By the late 1970s, it was labelled contemporary Christian music (CCM) in an effort to broaden its appeal and image.

The following quote summarises the Jesus People Movement and the spiritual revival that seemed to come from nowhere: 'The movement—for lack of a better word—is raging across the nation like a wind-driven brush fire, jumping any obstacle to break out—almost by spontaneous combustion—in dozens of places, in dozens of forms … this is revival spirit unprogrammed, with no mission board strategies, no super-evangelists at the head.'[6]

Larry Eskridge, in his comprehensive book *God's Forever Family: The Jesus People Movement in America,* underlines that the Jesus revolution changed the Christian church significantly, particularly the larger evangelical subculture, paving the way for a more relational and expressive style of worship and reaching out to the wider community. For a succinct summary of the Jesus People, it's worth reading a shorter article by Eskridge published in *The Conversation* titled '"Jesus People"—A Movement Born from the "Summer of Love"'.[7]

What Billy Graham Said about the Jesus People Movement

As the Jesus People Movement gained momentum across the US and further afield, many Christian leaders were trying to work out if this was a genuine move towards God. Huge doubts arose, as these young Jesus People seemed to have no respect for the house of worship by entering barefoot, not bathing or getting a haircut and playing their strange folk music. Some even started Christian communes. Christians called on Billy Graham, the man that most American Protestant Christians trusted and respected.

Billy Graham had been observing the Jesus People phenomenon for a while and had already begun to write a book about it. He published *The Jesus Generation* in 1971, shortly after the *Time* magazine exposé.[8] Graham made some very good observations, stating that the Jesus People Movement was not without its pitfalls and critics. 'Some say it is too superficial—and in some cases it is. Some say it is too emotional—and in some cases it is. Some say it is outside the established church—and in some cases it is. But even in the early church such problems were encountered'.[9] He also said it was interesting that it seemed to be spontaneous, with no single leader. He listed nine admirable characteristics that stood out to him:

THE NEXT REVOLUTION

1. It centres on Jesus.
2. It's Bible-based.
3. It demands an *experience* with Jesus Christ.
4. It puts a renewed emphasis on the Holy Spirit.
5. Young people are 'finding a cure for drugs and other vicious habits which increasingly are captivating and enslaving the youth of the world'.[10]
6. It emphasises Christian discipleship. Quoting *Time* magazine from 21 June 1971, the movement embraces 'the most persistent symbol of purity, selflessness, and brotherly love in the history of Western man'.[11]
7. It involves a strong sense of social responsibility.
8. There is an incredible zeal for evangelism. Quoting *Time* magazine again: 'They are afire with a Pentecostal passion for sharing their new vision with others. Fresh faced, wide-eyed young girls and earnest young men badger businessmen and shoppers on Hollywood Boulevard, near Lincoln Memorial in Washington, in Dallas, in Detroit, and in Wichita, witnessing for Christ with breathless exhortations.'[12]
9. It has a reemphasis on the second coming of Jesus Christ.

Billy Graham used the 'one way to Jesus' hand sign characteristic of the Jesus People on a number of occasions, which people interpreted as a sign of support for the movement.

Interestingly, he stated:

> What secular media was just finding out had already been going on for several years. Various organisations working with young people, such as Fellowship of

Christian Athletes, Campus Crusade for Christ, the Intervarsity Christian Fellowship, Young Life, Youth for Christ, the Navigators and many others, had already found that young people by the thousands were turning to Christ. Young evangelists began to emerge, preaching the Gospel in the contemporary language of modern youth.[13]

After describing the characteristics of the Jesus People, he then explained that even though thousands of young people were turning to Christ, it was still only a minority. 'The vast majority of young people are still alienated, uncommitted, and uninvolved.'[14]

John Lennon was proven a false prophet by overwhelming evidence that Christianity did not shrink and die. But he did have a point about the state of its followers.

The Fire Burns Out

The Jesus People Movement lasted around a decade before fading out.

So, what happened? This is the million-dollar question.

In his excellent history of the Jesus People Movement, Larry Eskridge wrote a whole chapter titled, 'I Wish We'd All Been Ready'. Of course, the young people of the Jesus revolution got older, had children of their own, and have now become grandparents. If I had a dollar for the number of older people I've met who were converted during this incredible revival, I'd be rich. Many have gone on to lead churches and ministries, and the zealousness and warmth of their faith is still there. But every generation needs its own revival.

Eskridge mentioned that in addition to Christian contemporary music, the boom in Christian bookstores, merchandising, broadcasting, and entertainment (like *Veggie Tales* and the wider acceptance of youth culture and Christian rock) were a result of Jesus People's influence.[15]

The Jesus revolution arrived like a tsunami. When it hit, it seemed few were ready. Not only were churches not ready, but a lot of time was spent trying to decide if this was indeed a move of God. There was a great deal of judgement on the outward—the clothes, hair, communal lifestyle, music, and so on. This created a significant barrier. There was a fear of the Jesus Freaks, of them influencing or 'infecting' other young people in the church. It appears that while many churches were grappling with these questions, the Jesus revolution came and went. An ex-hippie Jesus freak, now a leader in a Christian parachurch organisation, told me that if churches had been ready, then the impact would have quadrupled in reaching young people with the gospel.

Purity, Selflessness, and Brotherly Love

The secular *Time* Magazine article described the Jesus People with three outstanding characteristics: 'purity, selflessness and brotherly love'. These were also outstanding characteristics of the early church, and from what I read, the persecuted church today. We hear story after story emerging from the underground church in Asia, Eastern Europe, and the Middle East where Christians are closely knit. They stand with each other in the most adverse circumstances of severe persecution and risk. They are the counter-culture.

The question we have to ask is how we would describe today's Western Christians. Regarding purity, the church has been ravaged by pornography and sex scandals. Christian marriages break down at the same rate as non-religious marriages. Regarding selflessness, Western Christians have become consumers of Christianity for self-improvement, therapeutics, or a sense of belonging. And brotherly love, what of it? We are more divided and disconnected than ever.

To deny self and radically follow Jesus, the next Jesus revolution surely must be born within the hearts of Christians. May the Lord bring revival to his church in the West so that they begin to manifest *purity, selflessness, and brotherly love.*

---

1. Jordan Runtagh, "When John Lennon's 'More Popular Than Jesus' Controversy Turned Ugly" *Rolling Stone*, July 29, 2016, https://www.rollingstone.com/music/features/when-john-lennons-jesus-controversy-turned-ugly-w431153.

2. See Eskridge's book for a more comprehensive overview: Larry Eskridge, *God's Forever Family: The Jesus People Movement in America* (Oxford: Oxford University Press, 2013).

3. Larry Eskridge, "'Jesus People' – A Movement Born from the 'Summer of Love.'" *The Conversation*, September 15, 2017, https://theconversation.com/jesus-people-a-movement-born-from-the-summer-of-love-82421.

4. James Maloney, *Ladies of Gold: The Remarkable Ministry of the Golden Candlestick, Volume 1* (Bloomington, Indiana: WestBow Press, 2011).

5. Jessica Russell, "Chuck Smith and the Jesus Movement," *Calvary Chapel* magazine, July 15, 2020, https://www.calvarychapelmagazine.org/index.php/calvary-chapel-articles/499-the-jesus-movement.

6. Eskridge, *God's Forever Family*, 4.

7. Eskridge, "Jesus People."

8. Billy Graham, *The Jesus Generation* (London: Hodder and Stoughton, 1971).

9. Ibid., 16.

10. Ibid., 18.

11. Ibid., 19.

12. Ibid., 20.

13. Ibid., 15.

14. Ibid., 22.

15. Eskridge, *God's Forever Family*, 249–251.

— 2 —

Philosophies That Fuelled the Counter-Culture

The Jesus revolution was just one of the revolutions and movements that exploded during the '60s and '70s. And although it touched thousands upon thousands of young people, it did not impact the vast majority, as Billy Graham rightly noted. Something was going wrong because young people, specifically those in the baby boomer generation, were breaking out and rebelling like never before. The world was at war as the Cold War and Vietnam raged. Man walked on the moon. The H-bomb was being tested. Psychedelics, rock music, and eastern mystical ideas abounded and fed the growing tumult. Young women were burning their bras and demanding sexual freedom while the generation before them, the silent generation (those born between 1928 and 1945) looked on in bewilderment.

The following chapters examine the revolutions and movements of the time and also take a glimpse at the progression of those ideas, carried by the baby boomers to what we see manifest today. And what we see is selfism or the cult of self, but I'll get to that later.

First, it is helpful to define revolutions and movements, as this is important to fully appreciating the historical events in this book.

Philosophies That Fuelled the Counter-Culture

Revolution: 'A radical and pervasive change in society and the social structure, especially one made suddenly and often accompanied by violence.'[1]

Movement: 'A group of people working together to advance their shared political, social, or artistic ideas.'[2]

Revolutions and movements are grouped together in political studies. They are activities that happen outside political mechanisms, and they involve mobilising people to take action to bring about change. Movements can lead to revolutions. Throughout this book, I'll be using 'revolutions' and 'movements' interchangeably.

One of the aims of this book is to help understand how we got to this place because we are seeing that many young people today are perplexed. They look around at a world where there are no structures, no objective truth, broken families, political polarisation, and uncertainty. Institutions such as religion and civil society are in decline and mocked, and there is so much disunity. Many young people are seeking to retrace steps to solid structures such as the foundational Judeo-Christian faith, particularly the traditional expression found within Orthodox churches.[3]

To retrace steps takes some courage and I admire the many young people who are doing so. Of course, to retrace steps, one needs to go further back than the '60s and '70s, even back to the garden of Eden—where there were lies, deception, and the appeal for *self* to become like God.

There is nothing new under the sun. For this book, it is enough for the present to go back to the time when the accelerator was pressed to the floor—when the boomer elites drove like Jehu through our institutions with their agenda.

Before continuing though, it's necessary to examine philosophies that greatly influenced the idealistic boomers and led to the dismantling of our ancient traditions of family, religion, and civil society. This left a void that caused people to think there was no other purpose beyond self.

That said, this chapter was hard to write, and I tried strenuously to avoid it for fear of harping on about something that young people are hearing constantly from the more conservative, cultural critics in the West. But the more I researched the era of the '60s and '70s, the more I discovered that the 'new' ideas hippies embraced with enthusiasm and idealism have had a devastating effect on future generations. This chapter will help you make sense of all of the following ones and equip you to discern the ideas that are flooding our culture today.

Philosophies

There's a sign on an Anzac war memorial in my little rural town that makes me stop and ponder every time I pass: 'The price of freedom is eternal vigilance.' It's believed to have originated from a speech by Irish lawyer John Philpot Curran in 1790: 'The condition upon which God hath given liberty to man is eternal vigilance.' [4]

When a military force goes into battle, they have to understand the topography of the war and the methods of the enemy or the battle may be lost. We are in a spiritual war, and according to God's Word, our enemy is the Father of Lies. His most powerful weapon is deceit; thus, we need to be constantly vigilant, *eternally vigilant*, to filter ideas that come our way to determine if they are truth (and contribute to human flourishing and freedom), or if they are lies (that will lead us astray and into bondage).

The Bible instructs Christians: 'See to it that no one takes you captive through hollow and deceptive philosophy, which depends on human tradition and the elemental spiritual forces of this world rather than on Christ' (Colossians 2:8 NIV).

As Christians, we must be diligent to examine philosophies from human thinking that inform us about the world around us, how we relate to one another, how we govern, and how we view our religion, art, history, science, literature, and language.

The Most Influential Philosopher of Our Time

One of the most important philosophers who has influenced the world today is the German philosopher Karl Marx. His ideas have been changing the world view of generations of young people through the education system and through the media and elites of our now post-Christian Western world. However, since many of us were inadequately educated in history, particularly younger generations, we are unable to recognise the empty philosophies of Marx that have been directing much of our culture today. These philosophies have focused on dismantling the basic roles and institutions of our society (like marriage, family, religion, fatherhood, motherhood etc.) and inverting people's attitudes towards them to the point that these institutions are mocked and held in low regard by the elites and *enlightened* of this generation. In the '60s and '70s, Marxist philosophies informed many of the revolutions and movements of the day, from the sexual revolution and the feminist movement to the antiwar and environmental movements, and we are seeing the fruit of these today.

To really understand the Marxist philosophy, we have to start with the man.

Karl Marx lived during the 1800s and died in 1883 at the age of sixty-four. Even though he studied philosophy and had no training in economics or politics, his political and social ideas impacted the world. Marx was from a Jewish family whose father had converted to Christianity for practical and social reasons. This provided more opportunity for him than the Jews living in Germany at the time. Marx became a devout atheist. His seething hatred and bitterness towards religion—namely Christianity and the Jewish faith—permeated his ideology and became what could be argued driving forces in his life.

The distinctive thing that stands out about Marx is his personal life. Even though he was married with children, his family were often destitute because he didn't work. He mostly lived on handouts from his parents, who eventually turned off the supply and relations soured. He was also supported significantly by his friend Friedrich Engels, who co-wrote their famous work *The Communist Manifesto*. Marx wrote other pieces including poetry, some very dark. A few even indicated that he'd sold his soul to the Devil and was doing the Devil's work.[5]

> *Till heart's bewitched, till senses reel:*
> *With Satan I have struck my deal.*
> *He chalks the signs, beats time for me,*
> *I play the death march fast and free.*[6]

I encourage you to read more about the man who is said to have been 'one of the most significant influencers of the modern world'.[7] In particular I recommend Paul Kengor's book *The Devil and Karl Marx*, which extensively covers many aspects of Marxism including its far-reaching impact on the Western world.

Marx's work, *The Communist Manifesto*, called for a new order of society. The current order—where people or groups owned private property and could worship and associate and hold opinions freely—would end. All of the structures that supported a society would need to be dismantled and restructured. This would then allow equity and the proletariat (the working class) could experience economic and social equity.

Marx believed that all structures in a society were developed and imposed by the ruling class, the bourgeoisie, who had the power and money to live well. Marx believed these structures kept the poor down and oppressed them, denying them the ability to get ahead in life. They also kept the ruling class, the rich, in their high positions.

The Russian Bolsheviks Implement Marxist Philosophy

The structure of society in Russia at the time was one ruled by czars and the majority of people were peasants, many of them living in poverty. Russia was kept back from progress and was very much undeveloped compared to its European neighbours (in light of the Industrial Revolution). It was a country suffering from centuries of imperialist rule with a massive, ill-treated underclass, the peasantry. The Russian Revolution in 1917 ended the rule of the Romanov dynasty. The people had continually cried out about their exploitation and called for reform. Even the Orthodox church had failed the people. So, when the Bolsheviks (led by Vladimir Lenin) grabbed power, ending the structure and tradition of imperialist rule, the change was welcomed with celebration and hope. The Bolsheviks became the Communist Party of the Soviet Union.

Although aspirations to rid society of the systems of oppression were in essence good aspirations, the imposed solution of Marxism had devastating consequences and caused great upheaval in the Soviet Union. How was the government to seize property and valuables from private citizens—from those who owned little to those who owned much? How could the government take from and control religious groups and their places of worship, such as churches, cathedrals, and temples? How could they take over all businesses—from manufacturing to farming—especially those that were passed down from generation to generation? Or take from those who had worked so hard to start up a family business? How would they rid the nation of private property? How could a government purge a nation of the opiate of the people—their religion—which held a different world view, one that looked to God as Saviour and not the state? This new order needed total control, not just of the means of production but also of the very souls of its citizens. They must be totally owned by the state and dependent on the state both physically and ideologically.

A single-party, absolute government was required for the Marxist ideas to be implemented. Everything had to be subject to the state, even the opinions or private thoughts of its citizens. In other words, totalitarianism was implemented—a system of government that is central and dictatorial, and its citizens are subservient to the state.

There would have to be a struggle, a revolution, violence and some casualties, but this would be for the ultimate good. People who disagreed must be cancelled, publicly disgraced, re-educated, removed from influence, locked away, or even destroyed.

And this is what happened in the Soviet Union under Stalin; in China under Mao Zedong; in North Korea under the Kim dynasty; in Cuba, Vietnam, and Cambodia. It is conservatively estimated that over 100 million lives were lost. Some have said that this was the greatest plague in human history.

Many of those who died in the Soviet Union were in gulags, prison camps of forced labour and re-education. Millions were sent to these gulags from the 1920s until the late 1950s, some simply from holding an opinion that the government didn't like. The Gulag system was mostly unknown until Aleksandr

Solzhenitsyn published his book *The Gulag Archipelago*. He was imprisoned in 1945 for eight years for criticising Joseph Stalin in private letters that he wrote to a friend whilst serving in the Red Army during the Second World War. He was one of the hundreds of thousands of 'political' prisoners who were tortured, interrogated and imprisoned as counter revolutionaries. His opinions were considered dangerous, and for the good of the collective, this citizen's thoughts and opinions had to be policed and controlled.

Many Christians have heard of Pastor Richard Wurmbrand, who suffered unimaginable cruelties and abuse in Romanian gulags. He wrote a book about his experiences titled *Tortured for Christ*. Christians were a target of particular hatred and vicious treatment in these prisons and labour camps. The accounts of torture inflicted on Christians, in order that they renounce their faith, are not reading for the faint-hearted. But they are necessary to see what evil governments via propagandised citizens can inflict on other citizens, and to make sure it doesn't happen again. Young people need to know this because if they believe they are inherently good and can form their own morals, then they become ignorant to their propensity for evil, and this is dangerous.

> What Russia's young artists, intellectuals and cultural elite hoped for and expected [as they led this revolution] was the end of autocracy, class division and religion, and the advent of world liberalism, equality and secularism. What they got instead was dictatorship, gulags, and the extermination of free speech and expression. Communists had sold their ideology to gullible optimists as the fullest version of the thing every modern person wanted: Progress.[8]

They were the young progressives, *liberal* progressives.

Aleksandr Solzhenitsyn summarised the decline of the former Soviet this way:

> If I were asked today to formulate as concisely as possible what was the main cause of the ruinous Revolution that swallowed up some 60 million of our people, I could not put it more accurately than to repeat: "Men have forgotten God; that's why all this has happened."[9]

The Long March through the Institutions

After the Russian Revolution in 1917, Communists believed that the workers of the world would rise up in Western nations, seize power and implement communism, particularly after WWI. The reason they needed to revolt was because Marxists believed that Western workers were oppressed by the ruling class and there was gross inequality.

But the workers of the West did not rise up. Since communism's goal was always global, with ideas of worldwide revolution and worldwide government, Marxist theorists started to rethink 'how they could achieve world revolution and world government now that the Western working class had abandoned the idea'.[10]

A leading Marxist intellectual after WWI, Antonio Gramsci, put his mind to understand why Marx's ideas hadn't taken off in the West. He came to believe that it was because of the strong institutions of civil society such as the family, the church, trade unions, and the education system that reinforced capitalist ideas in the masses.[11] The thinking was that the people in the Western capitalist system of government were under 'false consciousness', not realising that they were being oppressed by the capitalist system.

Lenin and Stalin, leaders in the Russian communist revolution, and other early Marxists, believed that the economic system would determine culture. However, Gramsci and other Marxist intellectuals from the Frankfurt School in Germany believed this was the wrong way around, that *culture* would determine *economics* or politics. '*Otherwise put, culture is not downstream from economics, but economics is downstream from culture.*' [12]

Theological lecturer Rob Smith explains in his article 'Cultural Marxism: Fact or Fiction':

> The significance of this inversion of classical Marxism is profound. What it means is that if you want to change the economic structure of society, you must first change the cultural institutions that socialise people into believing and behaving according to the dictates of the capitalist system. The only way to do this is by cutting the roots of Western civilisation—in particular, its Judeo-Christian values, for these (supposedly) are what provide the capitalist root system. In short, unless and until Western culture is dechristianised, Western society will never be decapitalised. How might this be accomplished? By an army of Marxist intellectuals undertaking (what was later called) "the long march through the institutions of power"; that is, by gradually colonising and ultimately controlling all the key institutions of civil society. As Gramsci put it, "In the new order, Socialism will triumph by first capturing the culture via infiltration of schools, universities, churches and the media by transforming the consciousness of society." [13]

So how did all of this thinking from the Frankfurt School in Germany get to other nations? Pretty much all of these leading Marxist intellectuals were Jews, and during WWII many fled with their socialist ideas to the US, where 'in 1935, the Institute for Social Research affiliated with Columbia University, New York City. The school did not return to Frankfurt until 1951'.[14] These ideas spread to other universities across the nation, and the boomer generation university students went on to carry them to the next generations through academia, government, and the entertainment industry.

One of the significant developments of the Frankfurt School was critical theory or critical justice theory which when implemented encompassed 'unremitting criticism of any aspect of Western culture that was deemed to be oppressive or dehumanising, but short on constructive proposals'.[15] This was true to Gramsci's belief that the fundamentals of our traditional Western culture had to be exposed, criticised, and changed.

In addition, the Frankfurt School combined the teachings of Marx and Sigmund Freud, and under this influence, they 'understood that appealing to the masses' feelings was much more important than appealing to their reason'.[16] Therefore, the messages of fighting against oppression, social justice and equality went deep. And as others have highlighted, once someone reaches a belief based upon emotion, then it is very difficult to use facts to change their opinion.

> The appeal to emotion is a logical fallacy that occurs when a misleading argument, and particularly one that is unsound or missing factual evidence, is used with the goal of manipulating people's emotions ... The appeal to emotion can be highly effective as a rhetoric technique, due to the nature of human cognition. This is because, when people process information and make decisions, they often rely primarily on their intuitive,

emotional response to things, rather than on a logical, fact-based reasoning process.[17]

In addition, in his article titled, 'What is Cultural Marxism?', Bradford Hanson explains:

> One of the most influential publications by the Frankfurt School was *The Authoritarian Personality* by Theodor Adorno. The book is a polemic against "prejudices and discrimination", chiefly of White people's "discrimination" towards Blacks. It was succeeded by ... [a] feminist revolution, which was aimed at Western men. White heterosexual men were cast as arch villains and were accused of racism, sexism, homophobia and so on, with the ultimate purpose being to destroy white Western civilisation'.[18]

As we have seen over the last years, the everyday White male in Western nations—grandfathers, fathers, uncles, brothers, and sons—is now looked upon with disdain. There has surely been a cultural war on boys and men. According to the critical theory idea, White males have been born into a capitalist system that favours them and they must be stripped of their advantages. They have been demonised, particularly the middle-aged White male, who was supposedly born in an era steeped in *privilege*.

The Great Refusal

Marxist intellectual Herbert Marcuse, in his 1964 book, *One-Dimensional Man,* admitted to the negativity of critical theory and how it leaves people without hope:

> The critical theory of society possesses no concepts which could bridge the gap between the present and its future; holding no promise and showing no success, it remains negative. Thus it wants to remain loyal to those

> who, without hope, have given and give their life to the Great Refusal.[19]

What is the Great Refusal? It is the continual lifelong resistance to 'things as they are'—a theory of Marcuse. It is saying no to the capitalist system of oppression and noncompliance 'with the rules of a rigged game, a form of radical resistance and struggle ... based on a subjectivity that is not able to tolerate injustice'.[20]

Marcuse and the Frankfurt School brotherhood of intellectuals obviously had it in for Western society as they believed that all manifestations of aggression, oppression, racism, slavery, classism, and sexism that marked post-industrial society are due to capitalism. Marcuse even went so far as to call democracy 'the most efficient system of domination'.[21]

Smith explains that this view is 'simplistic and an indefensible misrepresentation of historical reality' and says that 'criticising an imperfect system when you have no idea how to build a better one is more than idealistic; it is irresponsible'.[22] Western civilisation has no doubt had its low points. Capitalism, too, has not done itself any favours with its propensity for corruption (as with all government systems around the world, not the least, communism—with its utopian promises and over 100 million senseless murders of its own citizens whilst trying to implement 'equality'). Humanity is sinful, and Smith believes that to demonise Western civilisation is very narrow-minded and unthankful. The utopian ideal, coupled with the constant resistance and negatively criticising so much of our current culture, has created continual tension. Smith concludes in his article that overall, the ideas from the Frankfurt School idealists are 'of hopelessness'.

Expressive Individualism

Together with the philosophies above, it is important to highlight the rise of expressive individualism. The history of this philosophy includes ideas from intellectuals such as Descartes, Rousseau, Nietzsche, Marx and even Charles Darwin. The term 'expressive individualism' reflects how we understand self and express our inner core or psychological self to others. Trevin Wax, in his article, 'Expressive Individualism: What is it?' explains it well:

> The key here is that the purpose of life is to find one's deepest self and then express that to the world, forging that identity in ways that counter whatever family, friends, political affiliations, previous generations, or religious authorities might say.[23]

The hopeful exhortations to *find your true self, follow your heart* and *you be you* very much reflect this ideology of expressive individualism. Trevin Wax provides seven summary statements from Mark Sayers's book *Disappearing Church* that the reader will recognise as a familiar mindset of young people, even those within the Christian faith.

1. The highest good is individual freedom, happiness, self-definition, and self-expression.

2. Traditions, religions, received wisdom, regulations, and social ties that restrict individual freedom, happiness, self-definition, and self-expression must be reshaped, deconstructed, or destroyed.

3. The world will inevitably improve as the scope of individual freedom grows. Technology —in particular the internet—will motor this progression towards utopia.

4. The primary social ethic is tolerance of everyone's self-defined quest for individual freedom and self-expression. Any deviation from this ethic of tolerance is dangerous and must not be tolerated. Therefore social justice is less about economic or class inequality, and more about issues of equality relating to individual identity, self-expression, and personal autonomy.
5. Humans are inherently good.
6. Large-scale structures and institutions are suspicious at best and evil at worst.
7. Forms of external authority are rejected and personal authenticity is lauded.[24]

The rise of selfism is a strong force in Western culture today, and it has been silently absorbed into the church. It has caused God's people to turn inward—to their detriment as you will see during the course of this book.

Michael Stafford wrote an insightful article in 2013 for ABC Religion and Ethics titled 'Christian resistance to the "Cult of the Self"'. He said:

> The Cult of the Self is at the centre of the various economic, social and environmental problems our society faces - from abortion to the decline of the family to growing economic inequality and even global warming.[25]

We must not underestimate the cult of the self as this has filled the void after God was removed from our Western society.

From Boomers to Gen Z

Many of the incredibly grounding and stable institutions were criticised, deconstructed, and hollowed out over the decades by the invasion of ideas introduced en masse to the young boomers at universities and through the arts and entertainment. Helen Andrews, journalist, and author of the book *Boomers: The Men and Women Who Promised Freedom and Delivered Disaster*, said this in an interview about how the idealistic boomers failed to pass on to following generations the stability they enjoyed themselves:

> The Boomers themselves came of age at a time when religion was still functioning, civil society was still functioning, and they were the ones who threw off religion and said "I don't care about churches, I don't care about marriage." They got the best of both worlds. They got grounding in that stability that was still existing when they were growing up and they failed to pass it on to their children. So they had the stability then the liberation, where millennials did not inherit that stability, we just inherited chaos.[26]

I recently came across an example of inherited chaos that I believe we can all relate to. A young woman I know graduated with a teaching degree. Before entering university, she was a normal, happy, plain, everyday kind of girl. In a recent Facebook post, she had completely changed and was unrecognisable. She'd shaved half her hair and dyed it purple, announced her recent divorce (she'd married in her first year of university), and ranted angrily about how gross 'ableist and racist practices' permeated her education. She was 'disgusted by the inequality and inequity' of the modern-day education system with their 'unethical practices' built for 'rich, White people to succeed'. She also announced that she now has new pronouns, and she was 'feeling safe' after a brief stint in hospital after a mental health crisis.

This young woman proclaimed to now be free of the structures of oppression (like marriage and gender). Sadly, her rhetoric belies the obvious that she is indoctrinated in the woke 'conscious raising' ideology of Marxist philosophy that always produces the same fruit—bitter, angry and unhappy individuals who are conditioned to *resist and struggle* every day against the invisible forces of oppression. They are unconsciously absorbing a world view with self as their ultimate authority.

And this is why scores of millennials are searching, retracing steps and looking for that lost stability. They can see that something is grossly wrong. The beloved church, the body of Christ, needs to ready itself, have a reformation, resist the cult of the self, and awake and arise in righteousness. The next revolution needs to be in each Christian heart to cast off the empty philosophies that are holding us back, dethrone self, and be the lighthouse on the Rock to guide the lost safely back to shore.

> *'Be watchful and strengthen the things that remain' (Revelation 3:2 NKJV).*

---

1. "Revolution," *dictionary.com*, accessed April 3, 2018. http://www.dictionary.com/browse/revolution.
2. "movement," *Lexico UK English Dictionary*, accessed April 3, 2018, https://en.oxforddictionaries.com/definition/movement.
3. Jacob Sparks, "Why are Young People Becoming Orthodox?" Engage Orthodoxy, accessed May 9, 2020, https://www.engageorthodoxy.net/contemporary-conversations/why-are-young-people-becoming-orthodox.
4. Robert Deis, "'Eternal vigilance is the price of liberty,'" This Day in Quotes, last updated January 28, 2018, http://www.thisdayinquotes.com/2011/01/eternal-vigilance-is-price-of-liberty.html.
5. Paul Kengor, *The Devil and Karl Marx: Communism's Long March of Death, Deception, and Infiltration* (Gastonia, North Carolina: TAN Books, 2020).
6. "The Fiddler," *Early Works of Karl Marx: Book of Verse*, "Wild Songs," transcribed for MEIA by jim.esch, accessed June 22, 2021, https://www.marxists.org/archive/marx/works/1837-pre/verse/verse4.htm.

7. Jonathan Wolff and David Leopold, "Karl Marx," *Stanford Encyclopedia of Philosophy*, first published August 26, 2003, substantive revision Mon Dec 21, 2020, https://plato.stanford.edu/entries/marx.

8. Dreher, *Live Not by Lies: A Manual for Christian Dissidents* (New York City: Sentinel, 2020), 48.

9. Aleksandr Solzhenitsyn, "'Men Have Forgotten God': Aleksandr Solzhenitsyn's 1983 Templeton Address," *National Review*, December 11, 2018, https://www.nationalreview.com/2018/12/aleksandr-solzhenitsyn-men-have-forgotten-god-speech.

10. Bradford Hanson, "What is Cultural Marxism?" *National Vanguard*, February 13, 2019, https://nationalvanguard.org/2019/02/what-is-cultural-marxism.

11. Rob Smith, "Cultural Marxism: Fact or Fiction?" *Eternity* News, August 18, 2021, https://www.eternitynews.com.au/opinion/cultural-marxism-fact-or-fiction.

12. Ibid.

13. Ibid.

14. Ibid.

15. Ibid.

16. Editorial Staff, "What is Cultural Marxism?" Nordic Resistance Movement, February 10, 2019, https://nordicresistancemovement.org/what-is-cultural-marxism.

17. "The Appeal to Emotion: Persuasion Through Feelings Rather than Facts," Effectiviology, accessed May 7, 2022, https://effectiviology.com/appeal-to-emotion.

18. Hanson, "Cultural Marxism?"

19. Smith, "Cultural Marxism."

20. Patti Ryan, "Marcuse and The Great Refusal," Research for Citizenship, October 11, 2011, https://researchforcitizenship.wordpress.com/2011/10/11/marcuse-and-the-great-refusal.

21. Smith, "Cultural Marxism."

22. Ibid.

23. Trevin Wax, "Expressive Individualism: What Is It?" the Gospel Coalition US, October 16, 2018, https://www.thegospelcoalition.org/blogs/trevin-wax/expressive-individualism-what-is-it.

24. Wax, "Expressive Individualism."

25. Michael Stafford, "Christian resistance to the 'Cult of the Self,'" ABC Australia, March 21, 2013, https://www.abc.net.au/religion/christian-resistance-to-the-cult-of-the-self/10099956.

26. Allie Beth Stuckey, "Blaming Boomers for Millennials' Problems | Guest: Helen Andrews | Ep 446," uploaded June 29, 2021, YouTube video, 47:10, https://www.youtube.com/watch?v=xZc6UHc54KE.

— 3 —

The Civil Rights Movement

Now that we've looked at the ideas that fuelled the revolutions and movements of the '60s and '70s, we move on to look at each of these individually. I start with the Civil Rights Movement.

Martin Luther King Jr, a Baptist minister, led the Civil Rights Movement of the 1960s, which is arguably one of the most successful social movements in the modern world. This revolution changed society for the better. Black southerners played a significant role, rightfully demanding full civil rights for Black citizens. Martin Luther King (MLK) paid the ultimate price for his activism and was assassinated in 1968. King's most well-known quote is, 'I have a dream that my four little children will one day live in a nation where they will not be judged by the color of their skin, but by the content of their character'.[1] One of the most outstanding characteristics one notices when studying MLK's work was that the civil rights activists were peaceful and respectable, regardless of having to stand in the face of incredible injustice. It succeeded and was embraced by the majority because it 'appealed not just to secular standards of social justice but to a higher moral code'.[2]

It is important to note that this revolution was led by a Baptist pastor motivated and guided by Christian values and principles. It also operated under principles of non-violence and respect.

This revolution was the third breakthrough against racial discrimination—after the abolition of the slave trade, which was also led by an outstanding Christian in the British parliament, William Wilberforce in 1807. Wilberforce, like MLK, believed the Scriptures that said mankind is made in God's image and equal before God. And that's what motivated Wilberforce to relentlessly continue his fight. His health gave out shortly after a major breakthrough, and he succumbed to influenza in 1833.[3] Neither Wilberforce nor MLK lived long enough to see the full effect of their struggle for justice.

The second breakthrough against racial discrimination was led by another outstanding advocate for freedom who most people know little about. His name was William Knibb, a British missionary sent to Jamaica. No doubt MLK was inspired by William Knibb and his fellow activists because he uses a form of a quote that was written on a plaque in Jamaica dedicated at Knibb's burial.

> 'The same God who made the white made the black man. The same blood that runs in the white man's veins, flows in yours. It is not the complexion of the skin, but the complexion of character that makes the great difference between one man and another.' So spoken on 1st August 1839 at a meeting of the Falmouth Auxiliary Anti-Slavery Society chaired by a black man.[4]

William Knibb was a contemporary of Wilberforce. As a British missionary, he and his wife were sent to Jamaica by the Baptist Missionary Society, where he saw the horrors of slavery firsthand. Knibb successfully advocated the British government for the Abolition of Slavery Bill, which took effect on 1 August 1834. Wilberforce ended the slave trade in the British Empire—the stealing and shipping Africans and others for buying and selling—but there was still much more work to be done. What of those who already owned slaves? They continued as they had been, in complete ownership of the slaves and their progeny and dictating their lives. Many slaves continued to suffer incredible cruelty and spent their entire lives in forced labour.

Knibb knew that 'the principles of Christianity and slavery are so entirely opposed to each other, that the only remedy for these evils is the immediate and complete extinction of slavery'.[5]

Although the goal was the complete abolition of slavery, the Slavery Bill had to be negotiated, and this was a first-step compromise. The compromise in the bill was that slavery was changed into a six-year apprenticeship. When completed, slaves should be absolutely free, and plantation owners would be compensated by the British government for their loss.

In 1988, William Knibb was posthumously granted Jamaica's highest civil honour, the Order of Merit. He was the first White man to be awarded this recognition in Jamaican history. Again, there was still much more work to be done by many, and Martin Luther King carried on that same work in the same spirit—through motivation and peaceful protests in the 1960s.

A Parallel Movement

At the same time MLK was leading the Civil Rights Movement, there arose another parallel movement composed of mostly young people who were discontent with the methods of nonviolent protests to combat racism. In 1966, the Black Power Movement was established with a different view of how to achieve change. Organisations such as the Black Panther Party, the Black Women's United Front, and the Nation of Islam grew their memberships and expanded their political and social agenda to achieve self-sufficiency, self-determination, equality, racial pride and economic and cultural programs. The Black

Power Movement was inspired by Malcolm X, a Black nationalist. Once a leader in the Nation of Islam movement, he fell out with the leader, Elijah Muhammad, and was assassinated by members in 1965. An articulate writer and speaker, Malcolm X educated himself during his time in prison as a young man. He increased the numbers of the Nation of Islam movement from 500, in 1952, to 30,000 in 1963.[6] His biography was distributed after his death and inspired young Black people to join Black power movements and seek more power for Blacks—economically, socially, and politically—rather than follow the MLK strategy of seeking integration into the White-dominated society.[7]

The cry of the mainstream Civil Rights Movement was 'We want freedom!' but the cry of the Black Power Movement was 'We want power!'[8] This difference put MLK at odds with the leaders of the Black Power Movement, as MLK *didn't see violence and separatism as a viable path forward.*[9] However, the Black Power Movement was gaining more followers due to the disillusionment of the slow pace of progress (with the Civil Rights Movement coupled with issues of the time, such as the Vietnam War).

After MLK was assassinated, people reacted. There were riots in more than one hundred US cities to demonstrate their incredible shock and grief and highlight their belief that his assassins were part of those against the Black Power Movement. Later the same year, at the Summer Olympics in Mexico City, two Black athletes—John Carlos and Tommie Smith—demonstrated Black Power Movement support by raising black-gloved fists in the air whilst standing on the medal podium.

By 1970 more militant leaders of the Black Power Movement arose, including the Black Panther Party. This was founded in 1966, a year after the death of Malcolm X, and it followed his revolutionary philosophy. The original name was the Black

Panther Party for Self-Defense, with the purpose of patrolling Black neighbourhoods to protect against police brutality.[10] The Black Panther Party later evolved into a Marxist group and advocated for a '10-point program of socialist revolution (backed by armed self-defence)'.[11] They called for the arming of all African Americans, exemption of African Americans from the draft, release of all African Americans from prison, and monetary compensation to African Americans for centuries of exploitation by White Americans.[12]

The Black Panther Party differed from other Black power groups in primarily two ways:

1. Other groups generally regarded all White people as oppressors, but the Black Panther Party distinguished Whites as either racist or non-racist. They allied themselves with those they perceived as more progressive non-racists.

2. Other groups generally viewed all Blacks as oppressed. Not so for the Black Panther Party. They viewed Black capitalists and other elites as exploiters and oppressors as well.[13]

Mainstream society viewed the Black power groups, especially the Black Panthers, as 'violent, anti-white and anti-law enforcement'.[14]

In 2020, Netflix released a documentary titled *Who Killed Malcolm X?* It gives an account of Malcolm X's life and the struggles of the time—from a grassroots perspective—by interviewing members of the Nation of Islam group who lived through that time. It provides eyewitness accounts that I found very enlightening regarding how people thought about issues of the time.

A New Black Power Movement—Black Lives Matter

The Black Power or Black Liberation Movement declined in the 1970s; however, the Black Lives Matter movement (BLM) rose to prominence in 2020. It was inspired by the Black Power Movement of the '60s and '70s, and its ideology is said to live on in the Black Lives Matter movement.[15]

BLM was founded in 2013 to fight racism and anti-Black violence, particularly perceived police brutality against Blacks. In 2020, the media coverage of the George Floyd incident—involving a Black man dying while being restrained by police—put BLM's cause in the headlines.

Even though Floyd had a violent criminal history, including aggravated robbery, nothing warrants that kind of death, and BLM activists said it was because he was Black.[16] The distressing incident of his arrest was captured on video by a bystander, and a selected section of the video was broadcast worldwide, which sparked large and violent protests across cities in America as well as worldwide. Even though medical specialists testified to the extremely high and lethal level of fentanyl in Floyd's bloodstream at the time of the arrest, and a court conferring that the incident was not racially motivated, one of the arresting police officers was convicted of murder. The narrative of a racially motivated and brutal police murder was used by BLM activists to immortalise George Floyd as a fallen hero of their cause.

The riots and protests were supported by media. One of the narratives picked up by mainstream media, BLM, and many politicians was that a disproportionate number of Black people were being shot by police whilst unarmed. This is an example of the power of emotionally motivating the masses regardless of facts. In a population of over 334 million in America, many people were led to assume that the numbers were in their thousands:

> According to the Washington Post database, regarded by Nature magazine as the "most complete database," 13 unarmed black men were fatally shot by police in 2019. According to a second database called "Mapping Police Violence", compiled by data scientists and activists, 27 unarmed black men were killed by police (by any means) in 2019.[17]

Millions of people worldwide rallied under the BLM banner with the desire to see an end to all racism in society. Many were unaware of the underlying philosophies and agenda of the BLM movement they were aligning themselves with, nor were they aware of the actual data about police violence.

Like the Black Panther Party, BLM is a movement which is philosophically Marxist. Co-founder of the online movement, Patrisse Khan-Cullors, stated in an interview that both she and co-founder Alicia Garza are trained Marxists.[18] Khan-Cullors stood down from her role of executive director of BLM in May 2021 after intense criticism.

The *Chicago Tribune* reported:

> Patrisse Khan-Cullors, co-founder of Black Lives Matter and a self-described "trained Marxist," is extremely upset with media outlets reporting on her $3.2 million portfolio of luxury homes, including one in ritzy Topanga Canyon, California, and another in Georgia with an airplane hanger …
>
> Khan-Cullors explained her Marxist training and ideology in an interview with Jared Ball of The Real News Network. "We are trained Marxists. We are super-versed on, sort of, ideological theories. And I think that

what we really tried to do is build a movement that could be utilized by many, many black folk."

Khan-Cullors says the focus on her homes "has taken away from where the focus should be — ending white supremacy." And Black Lives Matter, which says none of the money for her homes comes from BLM, blames, you guessed it, white supremacy, saying this is "a tradition of terror by white supremacists against black activists."[19]

Do not miss the significance of this: amassing wealth is ideologically opposite to the Marxist belief of taking wealth from the rich and redistributing it to lower classes. The BLM founders were back in the spotlight in 2022 for their secretive purchase of a 5.8-million-dollar mansion in California.[20]

BLM UK renamed itself Black Liberation Movement UK in September 2020 and gained legal status as a community-benefit society. In doing so, it received up to 1.2 million pounds in donations that year.[21]

BLM organisations today have expanded their agenda much further than that of even Malcolm X, who was a married family man, husband, father and protector of his home. He certainly did not amass wealth for himself—such as we are seeing in the current movement. Its agenda on the BLM website was removed after too much negative publicity, but Gatestone Institute's two-part report says:

> BLM states that it wants to abolish: the nuclear family; police and prisons; heteronormativity; and capitalism. BLM and groups associated with it are demanding a moratorium on rent, mortgages and utilities, and reparations for a long list of grievances. BLM leaders have threatened to "burn down the system" if their demands are not met. They are also training militias

based on the militant Black Panther movement of the 1960s.[22]

The Marxist philosophy drives racial division. Martin Luther King Jr. surely saw a different path to fighting racial injustice when he said, 'Darkness cannot drive out darkness, only light can do that. Hate cannot drive out hate, only love can do that.'[23]

The Social Justice Gospel

Racism does exist, and the Civil Rights Movement was necessary, but Christians need a biblical response to racism rather than the way our culture has responded through BLM.

African American theologian Voddie T. Baucham Jr., in his recent book *Fault Lines*, outlines critical race theory/social justice philosophies that are driving the current antiracism movements and sees them as the greatest threat to the gospel, and he is not alone. Many other pastors, including John MacArthur, do too.[24] Baucham's book is an excellent read to understand the social justice movement and what he calls the 'cult of antiracism'.

After the George Floyd incident in 2020, many Christians became divided on the issue. Not that one side was against racism and the other not; both were against racism. The problem was that many Christians had been watching with concern the rise of BLM and were resisting the pressure of the mainstream to publicly support them. Their reaction was not understood by other Christians who were not aware of critical race theory (CRT) and other ideological drivers of this movement. And this has caused tension.

Baucham explains that of the many anti-biblical doctrines of the cult of antiracism, perhaps the most disturbing is the belief that due to a person's whiteness, they contribute to the maintenance of racial injustice, and there is 'no way to get out of the game'.[25] This is in essence 'imputed guilt' from one generation to the next.

> Whereas Christians see Adam as the Federal Head of all mankind whom the guilt of original sin is imputed to all of mankind, the cult of antiracism sees the inventors of whiteness as the Federal Head of all white people through whom guilt is imputed in the form of white complicity.
>
> "Without confession to the sin of white racism, white supremacy, white privilege," contends *Sojourners* magazine founder Jim Wallis, "people who call themselves white Christians *will never be free* … from the bondage of a lie, a myth, an ideology, and an idol."

Baucham warns his readers that this sentiment is an affront to the gospel. 'For the law of the Spirit of life has set you free in Christ Jesus from the law of sin and of death' (Romans 8:2).[26]

The Marxist critical race theory and critical justice ideas are simply philosophies of man and fall far short of God's just requirements set out in Scripture. In fact, God's requirements are much higher and much more demanding. We must not only outwardly act justly to all mankind; our heart attitude must also be humble and loving, even towards our enemies or those deemed as 'oppressors'. No one is excluded from this requirement, no matter their race, gender, or identity.

> *'But if you show partiality, you are committing sin and are convicted by the law as transgressors'*
> *(James 2:9 ESV).*

1. SUCCESS Staff, "You Know 'I Have a Dream.' Here are 10 MLK Quotes You May Not Know," *Success* magazine, January 16, 2017, https://www.success.com/you-know-i-have-a-dream-here-are-10-mlk-quotes-you-may-not-know.

2. Camille Paglia, "Cults and Cosmic Consciousness: Religious Vision in the American 1960s," an expanded version of a lecture delivered on 26 March 2002 at Yale University, Harvard University, Arion 10.3–Rev 15, winter (2003), http://www.bu.edu/arion/files/2010/03/paglia_cults-1.pdf.

3. Tejvan Pettinger, "Biography of William Wilberforce," Oxford, last updated March 21, 2017, www.biographyonline.net, https://www.biographyonline.net/politicians/uk/william-wilberforce.html.

4. Alan Jackson, "William Knibb, 1803–1845, Jamaican missionary and slaves' friend," The Victorian Web, last updated 2003, http://www.victorianweb.org/history/knibb/knibb.html.

5. Ibid.

6. "Biography," Malcolm X, accessed January 4, 2021, https://www.malcolmx.com/biography.

7. Sarah Pruitt, "How the Black Power Movement Influenced the Civil Rights Movement," History.com, last updated April 16, 2021, https://www.history.com/news/black-power-movement-civil-rights.

8. Pruitt, "Black Power Movement."

9. Ibid.

10. Garrett A. Duncan, "Black Panther Party," *Encyclopedia Britannica*, March 4, 2022, https://www.britannica.com/topic/Black-Panther-Party.

11. Pruitt, "Black Power Movement."

12. Duncan, "Black Panther Party."

13. Ibid.

14. Pruitt, "Black Power Movement."

15. Carl C. Chancellor, "#BlackLivesMatter deeply connects to Black Power movement," *USA Today*, updated May 31, 2016, https://www.usatoday.com/story/news/nation-now/2016/02/01/black-lives-matter-black-power-movement/78991894.

16. Kate Sheehy, "George Floyd had 'violent criminal history': Minneapolis union chief," *New York Post*, June 2, 2020, https://nypost.com/2020/06/02/george-floyd-had-violent-criminal-history-minneapolis-union-chief.

17. K. McCaffree and A. Saide, "How Informed are Americans about Race and Policing?" Skeptic Research Center, CUPES-007, February 10, 2021, https://www.skeptic.com/research-center/reports/Research-Report-CUPES-007.pdf.

18. Soeren Kern, "Black Lives Matter: 'We Are Trained Marxists' - Part I." Gatestone Institute, July 2, 2020, https://www.gatestoneinstitute.org/16181/black-lives-matter.

19. John Kass, "Column: What was Marx's position on high-end real estate? Ask BLM's Patrisse Khan-Cullors," *Chicago Tribune*, April 15, 2021, https://www.chicagotribune.com/columns/john-kass/ct-black-lives-matter-houses-kass-20210415-5a7cspw3irbu3p6pmgjedknp74-story.html.

20. Joshua R. Miller, "Black Lives Matter used donations to buy $6 million Southern California home: report," New York Pos, April 4, 2022, https://nypost.com/2022/04/04/black-lives-matter-used-donations-to-buy-6-million-southern-california-home-report.

21. Ewan Somerville, "BLM given legal status as it officially adopts new name Black Liberation Movement UK," *i News*, October 24, 2020, https://inews.co.uk/news/uk/black-lives-matter-anti-racism-protests-black-liberation-movement-736859.

22. Kern, "Black Lives Matter."

23. Martin Luther King Jr., "*A Testament of Hope: The Essential Writings and Speeches*," Goodreads, accessed February 8, 2022, https://www.goodreads.com/author/quotes/23924.Martin_Luther_King_Jr_.

24. Voddie T. Baucham, *Fault Lines: The Social Justice Movement and Evangelicalism's Looming Catastrophe* (Washington, D.C.: Salem Books, 2021), 3.

25. Ibid., 76–77.

26. Ibid., 77.

— 4 —

The Psychedelic Revolution

The psychedelic revolution greatly influenced the baby boomer generation. Not that all young people took psychedelics (hallucinogenic drugs that induced altered states of consciousness), but the rock and roll artists they followed did. It was through their music that ideas spread, and these ideas were about freedom from traditional structures and about breaking out from authority.

> Drugs gave my generation vision. They allowed us to break through the conventions and formulas of the fifties. It was a tremendous, revolutionary movement. But over time, I have to say, drugs removed my generation from the ability to translate their vision into permanent, material form so that the vision could go on to maturation. The visions have been lost.[1]

So said Camille Paglia, an academic and a rebel of the counter-culture.

For sure the psychedelic revolution had a tremendous impact. Young artists poured their ideas into their music, which was the medium that carried pop culture ideas around the world.

This chapter not only looks at the psychedelic revolution, but it also examines the impact of drugs today, which is much more widespread. As you'll appreciate, this topic is both massive and complex, and this snapshot is far from adequate in covering the issue entirely.

LSD: 'Turn On, Tune In, and Drop Out'

First synthesised in 1938 by Albert Hofmann in Switzerland, LSD was thought to assist certain psychiatric conditions. It was trialled during the 1960s. But by 1968, it had been outlawed in America, with other countries following. It mostly became popular in America through a clinical psychologist by the name of Timothy Leary, who encouraged his students to 'turn on, tune in, and drop out'.[2]

Leary also co-authored the book *The Psychedelic Experience: A Manual Based on the Tibetan Book of the Dead*.[3] Along with his coauthors, he believed that psychedelic drugs enhanced consciousness (as opposed to morphine or alcohol, which dulled the consciousness) and encouraged the use of psychedelics amongst both students and other lecturers at Harvard. He was eventually dismissed but went on to give lectures at universities around the nation, encouraging students to experiment.

Academic Camille Paglia was a university student during that time, and this is what she said about LSD:

> I feel that the real visionary thinkers of my generation destroyed their brains on drugs. I think that LSD just leveled all the truly talented people of my generation ... My classmates. I think the authentic imaginations, the really innovative people of my generation, the most daring of my generation took the drug. Now I, for some reason, felt that the LSD was untested, and I did not want to experiment with it. But I was very interested in it. I was interested in all types of 'vision quests' at the

> time. I went up with fellow students [from SUNY-Binghamton] to see Timothy Leary speak at Cornell. I saw him, and it made me uneasy that he was the guru with such a crowd around him, but his face was already twitching. I could see that this was not going to end well, and it did not.[4]

Leary believed that taking psychedelic drugs in measured and proper doses should be legal for reasons such as spiritual revelation, union with God, personal growth, and self-development. Timothy Leary has an interesting history and is connected with many Hollywood and musical figures of today; it is well worth reading about him. Throughout his lifetime, he was incarcerated multiple times on drug possession, even once escaping from a low security prison with the help of his friends. Because of the ideas that he espoused, President Nixon described him as 'the most dangerous man in America', and a book of that title was released in 2018 retelling the story.[5]

In his 1983 autobiography, Leary records a discussion he had with writer and philosopher Aldous Huxley. One of the early pioneers of LSD, Huxley said: 'These brain drugs, mass produced in the laboratories, will bring about vast changes in society. This will happen with or without you or me. All we can do is spread the word. The obstacle to this evolution, Timothy, is the Bible.'[6]

Leary then follows with this:

> We had run up against the Judeo-Christian commitment to one God, one religion, one reality, that has cursed Europe for centuries and America since our founding days. Drugs that open the mind to multiple realities inevitably lead to a polytheistic view of the universe. We sensed that the time for a new humanist

religion based on intelligence, good-natured pluralism and scientific paganism had arrived.[7]

In the next chapter, I'll discuss Leary and Huxley's ideas further as they are significant.

President Nixon had his hands full with the Vietnam War and an increase of marijuana and LSD use amongst US college students and youth. By June 1971, he declared a 'war on drugs', believing it was public enemy number one. Marijuana was categorised as a Schedule 1 drug that carried the highest penalty, along with LSD. The use of LSD reached such proportions that by the end of 1968, it was banned in all states.[8]

Many claim their psychedelic trips as 'enlightenment' since it produces hallucinations, vivid colours, out-of-body sensations, feelings of euphoria to paranoia (depending on the individual), and a dissociation from reality.[9] Hence Leary's belief that it enhances consciousness by transporting one to another level, not unlike a virtual world.

Musicians in particular promoted drug use and admitted to writing songs while on acid trips. The popular Beatles' song 'Lucy in the Sky with Diamonds' was believed to be an acronym for LSD, although this was denied by Lennon.[10] Bands like The Grateful Dead openly promoted drug use and performed while under the influence of illicit drugs. Their audiences at concerts were also known to have enjoyed the entertainment while on drug trips. The band Pink Floyd had to let their founding member, Syd Barrett, go due to his prolific drug use and subsequent schizophrenia, which became a liability to the band.[11]

Smokin' Weed for Breakfast

Although much has been said about LSD, it is equally important to mention that the use of marijuana (cannabis) was a typical characteristic of the hippie era. The hippies' open consumption of weed, particularly during the '60s and '70s, was something that became a norm in public perception.

The Beatles were introduced to pot through an interaction with Bob Dylan in 1964.[12] One year later, at the height of Beatlemania, John Lennon said, 'The Beatles had gone beyond comprehension. We were smoking marijuana for breakfast. We were well into marijuana and nobody could communicate with us because we were just glazed eyes, giggling all the time.'[13]

Alcohol didn't seem to rate as strongly with hippies while marijuana was something of the foundation of day-to-day hippie existence. Eliza Berman writes in *Time* about this, quoting a *LIFE* magazine article from the 7th of July 1967: 'The soft sweet smell of marijuana hangs in the streets of San Francisco, New York, Atlanta, Detroit, Seattle. People pass on the sidewalk looking stoned, wearing buttons saying, "Turned On" or "Let's Get Naked and SMOKE".'[14] She goes on to say, 'So *LIFE* magazine described a cultural moment in which pot seemed to be taking over: readily available, encouraged by popular music, not merely a drug but the symbol of a revolution.'[15]

From music to art and even films, the use of hallucinogenic drugs by creatives in the '60s and '70s had a significant influence in this domain; however, as Paglia noted, the drugs hindered her generation from translating their visions into material form. Or did they?

Psychedelics and Drugs of the 21st Century

Inevitably, the West lost the war on drugs. Fast forward fifty years and we see that drug use has increased significantly, particularly the use of psychedelics:

The Psychedelic Revolution

Psilocybin [magic mushrooms], MDMA, LSD, DMT ... These are just the common psychedelics being consumed across the globe. Whether consumed for recreational use, spiritual pursuits, artistic inclinations, or therapeutic use, research estimates that over 30 million people are consuming psychedelics in America alone. Psychedelic research has come a long way since the discovery of the various varieties, however, there are a few individuals who are considered to be the pioneers of psychedelic research, two of which went down in history for their controversial Harvard Psilocybin Project.[16]

Those two individuals were psychologists Timothy Leary (of LSD-proponent fame) and Richard Alpert (aka Ram Dass), who were both fired from Harvard in 1963. (After a meeting with a guru in India, Alpert changed his name to the more spiritual Eastern name of Ram Dass, since his experience with taking psilocybin or magic mushrooms in Mexico led him to pursue new spiritual endeavours.[17])

Also a 21st century drug, marijuana or cannabis has been and is being legalised in states and countries across the globe.

Peter Hitchens, columnist with the *Daily Mail*, has done much research on the topic of drug use and criminal law. He wrote the book *The War We Never Fought*, referring to the supposed war on drugs by Western nations.[18] His concern is the connection between mental illness and cannabis as well as their direct links to crime. He is very much against the stupefying and apathetic effects it has on users and believes this is a moral issue.

It is worthwhile to read Hitchens' blog on this topic titled *Stupid Arguments for Drug Legalisation Examined and Refuted*, which provides many insights. He skilfully and factually discredits the arguments for the legalisation of marijuana (yes, even the one about reducing crime) in more entertaining detail.[19]

Along with Hitchens, Helen Andrews points the finger back to the boomer generation for today's drug problems:

> One in five white women on anti-depressants, and one in six of all Americans on some kind of psychiatric medication: this would not have been possible without the boomer era's broader embrace of mind-altering drugs.
>
> It is harder to say which is sadder, the number of people who have overdosed on heroin or the number permanently fuzzying their emotional perception of the universe because they were once sad enough to pop a positive on a PHQ-9. Most depressive episodes end on their own within six to eight months; prescriptions, unfortunately for patients, but fortunately for the manufacturers of Wellbutrin, last indefinitely.
>
> It is interesting to note how closely drugs have tracked the boomers as their needs and tastes have changed with age. Marijuana gave way to cocaine when they became old and rich enough to prefer "the champagne of drugs" (as The New York Times called it in 1974). On the legal side, the fad for Ritalin conveniently arose at exactly the right time to make the boomers' school-age children easier to manage.[20]

The widespread legalisation of marijuana is a result of the boomer drug revolution. Andrews writes caustically that we might even live to see the day when recreational street drugs might be covered by Medicaid, which would bring the boomer drug revolution to completion.[21]

Weapon of Mass Destruction—The Opioid Crisis

America is witnessing a drug crisis as never seen before. Currently, '11.7% of Americans [aged] 12 and over use illegal drugs' with 8.1 million of them having a drug disorder.[22]

More disturbing though is the evolving opioid crisis, especially during government lockdowns.[23] In the US, pandemic-period numbers estimate that 136 Americans die from an opioid overdose *every day*.[24] Don't miss this—136 souls needlessly perish per day. In the last twenty years, close to one million Americans have died from opioids.

Neurologist and psychologist Robin Nusslock explains how opioids work in the body:

> We all have opioid receptors in our brain and throughout the body. The opioid system in our brain is a gating mechanism that releases the opioids our body manufactures, such as endorphins, to reduce pain we feel. Taking opioids makes us feel good because it binds to receptors in our biology that, by design, give us pleasure. The opioids also lead to the release of a molecule called dopamine, which motivates us and gives us energy.

"All drugs ... eventually hijack the dopamine circuit in the brain," he explained. "The person becomes hyper-focused on getting the drug at the expense of other rewards in the environment."

Taking the drug goes from producing pleasure to a powerfully habitual necessity.

Additionally, stress triggers our brain's reward circuits. For example, we may crave donuts when we are stressed.

> For someone who is addicted to opioids, stress increases the brain's need for rewards and its craving for the drug.[25]

Fentanyl is an opioid; it is cheap and often mixed with other drugs like cocaine. In 2020 fentanyl-related drug overdoses surged to become the top US killer in adults aged 18 to 45. It has overtaken the previous top causes of death in that age bracket (suicide and vehicle accidents) according to the Centers for Disease Control and prevention (CDC) and a nonprofit group called Families Against Fentanyl.[26]

> Fentanyl is a synthetic opioid that's 50 to 100 times more potent than morphine, highly addictive, and deadly.[27]

James Rauh, from Families Against Fentanyl, said that 'America's young adults—thousands of unsuspecting Americans—are being poisoned'. He called for the federal government to 'declare illicit fentanyl a weapon of mass destruction', as doing so 'would activate additional and necessary federal resources to root out the international manufacturers and traffickers of illicit fentanyl and save American lives'.[28] [A weapon of mass destruction (WMD) is defined as 'any weapon that is designed or intended to cause death or serious bodily injury through the release, dissemination, or impact of toxin or poisonous chemicals, or their precursors'.[29]]

According to reports, the open borders have greatly increased drug trafficking from Mexico. Fentanyl is produced from chemicals supplied from China and is mixed with other substances to increase potency. It can also be pressed into counterfeit pain pills that look like Oxycodone, a prescription drug; these counterfeit pills are known as 'Mexican oxys'.[30]

In a Change.org petition, James Ruah of Families Against Fentanyl provides information comparing relative lethal doses per 158 lb. (approx. 72 kg) person: A lethal dose of Sarin nerve agent (a WMD) is .50 mg compared to just 2 mg of fentanyl.[31]

How much of this new trend of drug overdose is deliberate, we may never know. The world is watching, especially other Western nations, as these trends could become ours in the coming years.

A Biblical Response

One of the significant impacts of the Jesus revolution was that many hippies, even those from the hardcore drug scene, forsook their drug-taking lifestyle upon conversion and got *high on Jesus*. That phrase sounds somewhat shallow nowadays, yet whatever it was, when those lost, young people truly found Christ, they were transformed. Obviously a deep spiritual need was met when they understood the gospel and began to experience a new peace that was beyond human understanding.

At the time of writing, *The Jesus Revolution* movie is being filmed, retelling the story of this incredible movement. Jonathan Roumie plays Lonnie Frisbie, and he wrote this on his Facebook page:

> I can't tell you how honored I feel to be a part of The #JesusRevolutionMovie, playing the legendary, enigmatic hippie street-preacher Lonnie Frisbee (may he rest in peace).
>
> Lonnie was an essential part of this epic story based on true events that took place during the last great #REVIVAL in this country known as the "Jesus People Movement" or the "Jesus Revolution" (as @time magazine referred to it).

> He was particularly anointed by God with PROFOUND Gifts of the Holy Spirit, including the gifts of Healing and Prophecy among others. His contribution came at a watershed moment in American history where he effectively helped rescue vast numbers of the post-LSD tripping hippie youth who were lost, confused and disenfranchised, desperately seeking something greater than themselves. He convinced so many of his generation that the LSD and everything else they experimented with could not, and would never fill the void, provide answers or reveal the Truth.
>
> His answer - THE answer - was and is JESUS.
>
> As a result, untold numbers of kids -literally, teenagers- were brought to faith in Christ through his intense, magnetic witness in the late 60's and 70's, and he became a visual symbol of this movement whose epicenter was in Southern California and spread globally.[32]

During the Jesus revolution decade, scores of coffee houses were established for young people to hang out in. In the San Francisco Haight-Ashbury district, where over 100,000 young people gathered in the summer of love in 1967 and onwards, coffee houses sprang up with groovy names like 'The Living Room' and 'The Soul Inn'. These provided food and shelter and a place to sit and talk to others. Ex-hippies who spoke the hippie language displayed non-judgemental love and compassion towards the lost and won many to Christ through the ministry of those coffee houses.

Although we live in a different era, the needs are still the same, both practical and spiritual. The church must frankly and honestly address the issue of drug abuse, not once a year but continually. We must not only address the illicit drug taking but also those in our congregations who may be suffering with prescription drug dependency or alcohol abuse. Practically, the church can provide recovery programs that are Christ centred and filled with tough love and honesty.[33]

> In response to opioid use in their communities, churches ... have implemented 12-step recovery groups based on Christian teaching, while others sponsor suboxone clinics to support those in withdrawal. Other groups help addicts pursue cognitive-behavioral therapy or even aid those in need by providing foster care.[34]

In addition to these practical measures, according to physician Matthew Loftus, the spiritual worship aspect is significantly important in breaking addiction cycles, which he believes is rooted in sin. In an article he wrote for *Christianity Today*, 'Is Addiction a Disease? Yes, and Much More', Loftus said:

> The Church has an important opportunity here, not just in helping connect addicts in need with loving friendships, but also in re-centering us in our basic human purpose of worship.[35]

Not worship of self but worship of God.

What Loftus believes is that the root of the addiction must be addressed and that this is one of the most effective long-term solutions. And it begins in the heart.

> If addiction is even remotely an issue of misplaced affection, then for Christians, the gospel is the only suitable starting point. "All people—addicts in particular—are called to start with the gospel that satisfies our hunger, trusting in God's love for us and repenting of our sin," Loftus wrote. "Many people recover without trusting in Christ, yes, but those who are grasped by the gospel have a significant head start in

sorting out the 'hierarchy of loves' as they untangle the particular ways in which sin has created strongholds in their lives."[36]

As image bearers of Christ, we seek the physical and spiritual well-being of those around us, especially the weak. Saving those trapped in addiction and personal destruction is the role of the church.

The baby boomer war on drugs was lost, but the next generations must pick up that baton and carry the love and compassion of Christ to the hurting world.

---

1. Leslie Stackel, "High Times Greats: Interview with Camille Paglia," *High Times* magazine, April 2, 2020, https://hightimes.com/culture/people/high-times-greats-camille-paglia.

2. "LSD: A Short History," The Truth about LSD e-course, Foundation for a Drug-Free World, accessed May 6, 2022, https://www.drugfreeworld.org/course/lesson/the-truth-about-lsd/lsd-a-short-history.html.

3. Ram Dass, Timothy Leary, and Ralph Metzner, *The Psychedelic Experience: A Manual Based on the Tibetan Book of the Dead* (New York: Citadel Press, 1995).

4. Nick Gillespie, "Everything's Awesome and Camille Paglia Is Unhappy!" *Reason* magazine, March 19, 2015, https://reason.com/podcast/2015/03/19/everythings-amazing-and-camille-paglia-i.

5. Steven L. Davis and Bill Minutaglio, *The Most Dangerous Man in America: Timothy Leary, Richard Nixon and the Hunt for the Fugitive King of LSD* (New York: Grand Central Publishing, 2018).

6. Jeffrey Steinberg, "From Cybernetics to Littleton — Techniques in Mind Control," Schiller Institute, April 2000, https://archive.schillerinstitute.com/new_viol/cybmindcontrol_js0400.html.

7. Ibid.

8. History.com Editors, "War on Drugs," History.com, last updated December 17, 2019, https://www.history.com/topics/the-war-on-drugs.

9. Kathleen Davis, "The Effects and hazards of LSD," *Medical News Today*, June 22, 2017, https://www.medicalnewstoday.com/articles/295966.

10. Jordan Runtagh, "Beatles' 'Sgt. Pepper' at 50: Remembering the Real 'Lucy in the Sky with Diamonds.'" *Rolling Stone*, May 18, 2017, https://www.rollingstone.com/music/music-features/beatles-sgt-pepper-at-50-remembering-the-real-lucy-in-the-sky-with-diamonds-121628.

11. Samantha Richards, "The Influence of Drugs throughout Music in the 1960s: The Psychedelic Era," Longwood University Blogs, April 29, 2013, now archived.

12. Russel Cronin, "The History of Music and Marijuana (Part One)," *Cannabis Culture* magazine, September 8, 2004, https://www.cannabisculture.com/content/2004/09/08/3434.

13. Ibid.

14. Eliza Berman, "What the Panic Over Pot Looked Like in 1967," *Time*, 2015, now archived.

15. Ibid.

16. Chane Leigh, "Pioneers of Psychedelics Research: The Harvard Psilocybin Project and More!" veriheal, May 5, 2021, https://www.veriheal.com/blog/pioneers-of-psychedelics-research-the-harvard-psilocybin-project-and-more.

17. Ibid.

18. Peter Hitchens, *The War We Never Fought: The British Establishment's Surrender to Drugs* (London: Bloomsbury Academic, 2012).

19. "Stupid Arguments for Drug Legalisation Examined and Refuted," Peter Hitchens blog, *Mail on Sunday*, December 22, 2017, http://hitchensblog.mailonsunday.co.uk/2017/02/stupid-arguments-for-drug-legalisation-examined-and-refuted.html.

20. Helen Andrews, *Boomers: The Men and Women Who Promised Freedom and Delivered Disaster* (US: Penguin Publishing Group, 2021), chapter 1.

21. Ibid.

22. "Drug Abuse Statistics," National Center for Drug Abuse Statistics, https://drugabusestatistics.org.

23. Ellie Gardey, The Opioid Crisis Spikes Under Lockdown," *American Spectator*, June 6, 2020, https://spectator.org/opioid-crisis-lockdown-coronavirus/

24. "The Opioid Crisis: An 'Epidemic Within the Pandemic,'" Institute for Policy Research, Northwestern University, June 28, 2021, https://www.ipr.northwestern.edu/news/2021/opioid-crisis-an-epidemic-within-the-pandemic.html.

25. Ibid.

26. Eric Lendrum, "Fentanyl overdoses are leading cause of death for Americans ages 18 to 45," *Alpha News*, December 18, 2021, https://alphanews.org/fentanyl-overdoses-are-leading-cause-of-death-for-americans-ages-18-to-45.

27. Charlotte Cuthbertson, "Fentanyl Overdoses Become Leading Cause of Death in 18- to 45-Year-Olds," the *Epoch Times*, December 19, 2021, https://www.theepochtimes.com/mkt_app/fentanyl-overdoses-become-leading-cause-of-death-in-18-to-45-year-olds_4166280.html?v=ul.

28. Lendrum, "Fentanyl overdoses are leading cause of death for Americans ages 18 to 45."

29. Cuthbertson, "Fentanyl Overdoses Become Leading Cause of Death in 18- to 45-Year-Olds."

30. Ibid.

31. James Ruah, "Declare Illegal Fentanyl a Weapon of Mass Destruction," Change.org, December, 2020, https://www.change.org/p/u-s-government-declare-illegal-fentanyl-a-weapon-of-mass-destruction.

32. Jonathon Roumie, "Day 1 of a movie that's been years in the making....," Facebook, March 19, 2022, https://www.facebook.com/JonathanRoumieOfficial/posts/504521374577400

33. Ashley Abramson, "The Opioid Crisis Is the Life Issue Christians Must Address," *Relevant* magazine, October 27, 2017, https://relevantmagazine.com/current/the-opioid-crisis-is-the-life-issue-christians-must-address.

34. Ibid.

35. Ibid.

36. Ibid.

5

The New Psychedelics

Although it might seem somewhat out of place, this chapter explores another aspect of psychedelics that I believe is important and relevant; it highlights the innate hedonistic drive in man to pursue pleasure and avoid pain. And pain, also known as suffering, is unbearable without meaning.

Together with this, the chapter also highlights some of the forward thinking by Timothy Leary, in his writings from 1994, about what the new psychedelics of the future would look like. That was over twenty-five years ago. I'll let you be the judge as to whether his predictions have come to pass.

Aldous Huxley (1894–1963), a friend of Timothy Leary, was also one of the early pioneers advocating for 'brain drugs'. He was a generation older but very visionary for his time. His utopian novel *Brave New World*, written in 1931, sheds light on his ideas of how the world might look with psychological conditioning in a sophisticated, hedonistic society where suffering could be avoided. Although others wrote that his novel was 'satirical' and 'nightmarish' and 'exposing the aimlessness and emptiness' of the contemporary society, Huxley's association with Timothy Leary causes one to wonder if it was indeed Huxley's aim.[1] It is worthwhile to look at the vision of utopia or dystopia Huxley had in mind and compare it with what we see today—as it purports a vision of using drugs to help avoid suffering and pursue pleasure.

Aldous Huxley and His *Brave New World*

The novel is set in a futuristic society, called the World State, that is totally controlled through science and efficiency. Children are cloned and created outside the womb in a place called the Hatchery and Conditioning Centre. The infants then progress to a nursery and then a place for children to be raised, where they are indoctrinated against individuality and emotions. Children are 'socialised' to be sexually free because 'everyone belongs to everyone else' and hence, there are no families or family structure. Life is very comfortable in the World State, particularly since citizens are regularly provided with a drug called 'soma', taken in the form of small tablets that make them feel good. In larger doses, it creates *pleasant hallucinations* and a *sense of timelessness*. Anytime one has unpleasant feelings, one is encouraged to take soma, therefore unnecessarily avoiding emotional suffering. It is a world that has no poverty, sadness, or suffering of any kind; in fact, these things are strongly avoided.

One of the main characters is a young man they call John the Savage. He gets this name because he was rescued from one of the 'savage reservations', where the World State has not yet been implemented. On the savage reservation the culture, although living in primitive circumstances without the modern conveniences of the World State, still has traditional family structures, and promiscuity is looked down upon.

John's mother was supposedly lost whilst on a research project from the World State and therefore left behind on the reservation when she was pregnant with him. She raises him on the reservation within a traditional society with family structures in place. Turns out she may have been deliberately left there as she had become pregnant to a person of high standing, and women were not to get pregnant.

Life was tough for John growing up on the savage reservation. He was bullied and an outcast, being a child of a single mother who practiced the free love promiscuity that she was taught from her upbringing in the World State. John's mother had an old book by Shakespeare and taught him to read it. This enabled John to verbalise his emotions and reactions to his various situations, and it provided him a framework for his values.

Back in the 'civilised' World State, John struggles with the sexual norms, where he is laughed at as being uncivilised for not being sexually free. They find his language and the way he expresses himself peculiar, being influenced by his Shakespearian vocabulary. He hates the practice of taking soma, which he believes turns people into unthinking slaves, and he refuses to take it, to the astonishment of the people there. He eventually runs away and lives alone, drug free, in an isolated lighthouse until he is discovered.... I'll let you read the book to find out how it ends.

Huxley had incredible foresight into the future, considering he wrote his book in 1931. However, it leaves one questioning the philosophy behind Huxley's vision expressed in his novel.

The following excerpt from a lecture by Huxley provides a glimpse into how he believed the use of drugs could be the way to reorganise society:

> There will be in the next generation or so a pharmacological method of making people love their servitude and producing dictatorship without tears, so to speak. Producing a kind of painless concentration camp for entire societies so that people will in fact have their liberties taken away from them but will rather enjoy

it, because they will be distracted from any desire to rebel by propaganda, or brainwashing, or brainwashing enhanced by pharmacological methods. And this seems to be the final revolution.²

The New Psychedelics—the Technological Explosion and the Virtual World

Timothy Leary died in 1996, just five years after the development of the World Wide Web. Without experiencing the advances in technology that have rapidly progressed in the following decades, he surely had incredible insight:

> The second publication, Chaos and cyber culture, finds Leary in 1994, two years prior to his death, after decades as a divisive advocate of psychedelic drugs, altered consciousness, and transhumanism. Chaos and cyber culture is Leary's "cyberpunk manifesto", a treatise on the coming technology-obsessed generations and the new informational world they would inhabit. Leary's emphasis on establishing individuality and questioning authority is still in effect, but the vehicle he proposes is computer technology rather than mind-altering drugs.³

Don't miss it, the vehicle Leary proposes is computer technology rather than mind-altering drugs to establish *individuality* (free to do and be whatever I want without constraints and judgement, or selfism) and to *question authority* (the resistance to traditional structures). These young people will inhabit a *new informational world* and will be *technology-obsessed*. This will be a world that would replace psychedelic drugs in providing *altered consciousness* and *transhumanism*.

Don't miss the *transhumanism* bit as well, as this is gaining momentum in our technology-driven world with the rise of artificial intelligence (AI).

> Transhumanism is usually defined as a philosophical movement that advocates for the transformation of the human condition by developing sophisticated technologies to enhance human intellect and physiology, with the goal of overcoming fundamental human limitations such as suffering, decay, and even death. Basically, it is man improving himself by merging with technology.[4]

It is a philosophy that denies the root cause of most of the woes of humankind, is linked to the sinful nature in humankind, and is disturbing in what it will do if unchecked. The Scriptures teach us that redemption is available but not by technological means. The transhumanist movement is focused on 'extraordinary' men, whether they be the ruling class elite, a master race, or better human beings through technology (Elon Musk-type stuff), perhaps even, dare I say, extra-terrestrial creatures from another dimension—since the discussion of superhumans, UFOs, and extra-terrestrials is ramping up in this realm.[5]

Interestingly, the term 'transhumanism' was first used by Julian Huxley, the brother of Aldous Huxley. Julian was an evolutionary biologist and eugenicist, and the first president of the British Humanist Association, among other notable achievements.[6]

As man innately seeks and longs for immortality and an escape from suffering, corruption, and death, many are looking to technology for a biological upgrade. Transhumanism is a type of gospel, a hope for eternity. Christians yearn for immortality too; however, we seek it through the gospel, which promises resurrection from the dead and embodied immortality. As to the corruption issue of man, not only does the gospel address the state of our sinful soul here and now, but it also 'resolves it comprehensively after death'.[7]

In a later chapter, I discuss the phenomenon of this generation of digital natives and their perpetual connection to the virtual world of the internet. The 24-7 distraction is able to draw their minds or 'consciousness' away from present emotional distress or physical situations, not unlike soma. They can be outside their mortal bodies living a completely different life and experience—a bit like what is depicted in the Matrix movies. And as we all know, the virtual world and social media have an addictive or obsessive aspect, designed to continually capture one's attention.[8]

For a biblical response to transhumanism ideas and agendas, I recommend Sandra Godde's excellent book *Reaching for Immortality: Can Science Cheat Death? A Christian Response to Transhumanism*. But for now, it's time to move on to look at the spiritual revolution that was influenced greatly by psychedelics.

---

1. Britannica, T. Editors of Encyclopaedia, "Aldous Huxley," *Encyclopedia Britannica*, November 18, 2021, https://www.britannica.com/biography/Aldous-Huxley.

2. Steinberg, "Schiller Institute."

3. "The Works of Timothy Leary," Houghton Library, Harvard University, June 10, 2014, https://blogs.harvard.edu/houghtonmodern/2014/06/10/the-works-of-timothy-leary.

4. Contributed by Sandra Godde. For a more detailed account of some of the aspirations of the transhumanists, see Sandra Godde, *Reaching for Immortality: Can Science Cheat Death? A Christian Response to Transhumanism* (Oregon, USA: Wipf & Stock, 2022).

5. Paul D. Shinkman, "U.S. Releases UFO Report, Congress Criticizes 'Inconclusive' Findings,'" *U.S. News*, June 25, 2021, https://www.usnews.com/news/national-news/articles/2021-06-25/us-releases-ufo-report-congress-criticizes-inconclusive-findings.

6. Sean A. Hays, "transhumanism," *Encyclopedia Britannica*, June 12, 2018, https://www.britannica.com/topic/transhumanism.
7. Godde, *Reaching for Immortality*, introduction.
8. Erin Raupers, "The Addictive Nature of Social Media," healthy Penn State, March 16, 2018, https://sites.psu.edu/healthypennstate/2018/03/26/the-addictive-nature-of-social-media.

— 6 —

The Spiritual Revolution

With the psychedelic revolution in full swing, young people were exploring new realms of consciousness, and there was no stopping them. The spiritual realm was something that fascinated them and they were driven to explore it. As they threw off the bonds of the old, they eagerly sought new paths that would help them understand life. This chapter traces how the young baby boomers began to seek after other spirituality with gusto, one that did not require the moral constraints of traditional Christian morality, under which most of them were raised.

The '60s and '70s were a time of spiritual crisis and political unrest, not unlike today. The new religious vision of the day brought together spirituality from both the East and the West, and as mentioned previously, it was carried to young people across the world primarily through the medium of American pop culture, particularly through rock music and idolised rock stars.

Older generations (including parents of young adults who had lived through the Great Depression and World War II, not to mention the Korean War and the ongoing Cold War conflicts such as Vietnam and Cuba) didn't want their children to suffer deprivation, austerity, and insecurity the way they had. There was a swing towards materialism, which was something young people began to react against. But more so, they reacted to the veneer of order and composure that masked the underlying anxieties and uneasiness of the older generations. The values of uniformity and duty and the adherence to order provided a sense of security to the older generations, even a reassurance that all was well, even though they lived with a constant underlying threat of war.

Tens of thousands of young people drifted away from the traditions of their upbringing to explore alternative ways of navigating life and seeing the world. Since young people are supposedly more astute in detecting authenticity, it appears that they had a sense that all was not as it appeared. There seemed to be a crisis of meaning. In addition, according to Paglia, the many universities springing up around the United States were breeding radical activists who drew their teaching from the anti-Christian Marxist philosophy. They mixed their political beliefs with their Eastern religions, Native American influences, and occultic practices.[1]

The hippie culture of the '60s and '70s rejected and despised institutionalised religion—the rules, the morals, the hypocrisy, the straitjackets of performance, the unquestioning loyalty to traditions and institutions, the blind injustice—as they saw it.

Rejection of a higher power such as the God of Christianity leaves a spiritual void that will inevitably be filled by another form of spirituality or meaning.

Gurus and Pilgrims

It is not hard, then, to understand why the '60s and '70s was a time of exploring other spirituality, particularly Eastern religions and practices such as yoga, transcendental meditation (TM), Zen Buddhism, and Hinduism.[2] This spirituality looked attractive; it seemed to be peaceful and inward-looking, gentle, all-embracing, and meditative. It offered new experiences, paths, and ways of looking at the world.[3] Of course, the environment was ripe at the time with the simultaneous psychedelic revolution and the widespread availability of LSD and marijuana. Hippies considered drug use a type of spiritual experience, giving them the opportunity to explore different or higher levels of consciousness or reality or to open untapped areas of their mind. Paglia writes:

> Alteration of consciousness—"blowing your mind"—became an end or value in itself in the sixties. Drugs remade the Western world-view by shattering conventions of time, space, and personal identity. Unfortunately, revelation was sometimes indistinguishable from delusion.[4]

During this time, the Beatles were exploring alternative religions and first met the Maharishi Mahesh Yogi in London in 1967. At the peak of their popularity, they visited him in India to be instructed in meditation. They took photos with him, used the Indian sitar in their music, and caused a surge of interest in Eastern religions. Their fascination with Maharishi ended abruptly after he made sexual advances to a fellow celebrity pilgrim.[5]

The Hare Krishna cult attracted many young people, particularly hippies, many of whom eventually were forcefully rescued and returned to anxious parents.[6] Beatles member George Harrison wrote the catchy song in 1970 'My Sweet Lord' with the Hare Krishna refrain that helped to promote the Hare Krishna society worldwide.

Back to the Maharishi—his movement had significant following in the US. He founded the Spiritual Regeneration Movement, teaching a TM technique which took off around the world.[7] He was not only a spiritual guru of the Beatles but of many other celebrities, which gave the Maharishi an incredible amount of free publicity and endorsement. His goal was to teach TM as a way to spread love and peace throughout the world. This was particularly appealing to young people as they were in the midst of worldwide unrest. The Cold War and the Vietnam War seemed pointless and without an end.

The Spiritual Regeneration Movement reached a high during the '60s and '70s, and it continues to have a huge impact. Meditation is now considered a scientifically supported health program and not just a practice of Eastern mystics.[8]

Rabi R. Maharaj, son of a Brahmin priest, trained as a yogi from his early childhood and was expected to become a Brahmin priest like his father. As a young man, he had a radical conversion to Christianity during the time of the cultural revolution in the West, and he writes about his father:

> ... a trancelike state which he achieved through Yoga, used to be considered extremely peculiar and even a form of insanity to those unacquainted with eastern mysticism. However, "altered states of consciousness" have gained new acceptance in the West, beginning with drug experiments in scientific laboratories, and moving out into society until millions have now experienced this "alternate reality." Millions more have entered what is now called "higher consciousness" through hypnotherapy, autosuggestion, guided imagery and various forms of yoga popularized in the West from TM to "centering" and visualization. Moreover, there is a growing acceptance of the validity of psychic phenomena in the scientific community which has changed the former skepticism of materialistically orientated Western society into a new openness to the occult. We Indians, however, have known for thousands of years that there is real power in Yoga.[9]

As a boy, Rabi's mother explained to him what his father was doing in this trancelike state, she explained that his father was 'seeking the true Self that lies within us all, the One Being, of which is no other'.[10] After his conversion to Christianity, Rabi went to study in the UK and travelled throughout Europe. He recalls being astonished at the *Hinduization* of Western society and felt a responsibility to expose it.[11] But this importation of Eastern Mystical beliefs was also being facilitated by academics such as Aldous Huxley who had been 'experimenting for decades on how to translate Indian ideas into Western literacy and intellectual culture'.[12]

Cults and communes of all sorts proliferated during these turbulent years. Other groups that became infamous during the '60s and '70s attracted disaffected young people. These included those within the Rajneesh movement, whose followers were known as Rajneeshees or 'Orange People'. The Rajneesh denounced marriage as a social bondage and promoted free love and libertarianism.[13] Another cult was the American People's Temple, led by Jim Jones, who became internationally notorious after the mass suicide of about nine hundred followers in 1978 in Jonestown, Guyana, under his instruction.

Hippies and the Occult

Another important influence on the Beatles and other popular bands of the day was the late Aleister Crowley (1875–1947). Crowley was a Satanist and called himself 'the Great Beast'. He has a colourful history and wrote a number of books that no doubt could provide the content for a lifetime of nightmares. He led the pro-Nazi, German cult called the Ordo Templis Orientis.[14] In 1969 his autobiography was rereleased. The Beatles, in their apparent quest for enlightenment, appeared to be so influenced by his teaching that they inserted Crowley's face (back row, second from left) on the cover of their *Sergeant Pepper* album (1967).[15]

Paglia explains the degree of occultic influence on music of the '60s and '70s, including Crowley's:

> Because of its descent from blues—called the "devil's music" in the American south—rock already had a voodoo element lingering from Afro-Caribbean cults. But the Satanism in classic Rolling Stones songs and the magic pentagrams on Led Zeppelin's album covers and stage costumes came from Crowley. Jimmy Page, Zeppelin's virtuoso lead guitarist, collected Crowley memorabilia and bought his mansion, Boleskine House, on Scotland's Loch Ness ... Crowley admirers in seventies rock included David Bowie and heavy metal musicians like Ozzy Osbourne, whose song, "Mr. Crowley" ("You waited on Satan's call"), appeared in his first solo album after leaving Black Sabbath.[16]

Anton Szandor La Vey was another who cultivated Satanism in the '60s. He wrote *The Satanic Bible* (1970). Based in California, he too practiced and advocated Crowley's satanic black arts. He founded the Church of Satan in San Francisco with radical sexual liberation as a major aspect of his teaching. La Vey's home (6114 California Street) was painted black and visited by many celebrities. The house was believed to have once been a hotel. The Eagles popular song of the '70s, 'Hotel California' was 'believed to have been inspired by rites at La Vey's house'.[17]

The following observation by Camille Paglia gives a brief glimpse into the eclectic Eastern, occultic, and other spiritual influences of the '60s that went far beyond all boundaries set by the predominantly traditional Catholic and Protestant faiths of the day:

> ... demonstrations with a large hippie contingent often mixed politics with occultism—magic and witchcraft

> along with costumes and symbolism drawn from Native American religion, Hinduism, and Buddhism. For example, at the mammoth antiwar protest near Washington, DC, in October 1967, 'Yippies' performed a mock-exorcism to levitate the Pentagon and cast out its demons. Not since early nineteenth-century Romanticism had there been such a strange mix of revolutionary politics with ecstatic nature worship and sex-charged self-transformation.[18]

Yippies were a more radical group of the counter-culture. They were members of a new left-aligned group, called the Youth International Party, and were renowned for mixing their activism with mockery of any kind of institutional authority and revelry.[19]

The strong Eastern, pagan, and occultic influences, as well as anti-establishment mentality, set the foundations for future generations to experience a significant spiritual vacuum in the decades to come.

The New Age Movement

The unholy polygamous marriage between the spiritual beliefs of the East and the West, the occult, American Indian spirituality, pagan religions, nature worship, and others gave birth to the New Age movement. These themes were brought together in the counter-cultural movement of the day. No one has been able to exactly define the New Age thought, a Frankenstein of sorts; however, they have been able to provide some aspects of commonality. The following was taken from an article by Gavin McGrath titled 'The Significance of the New Age Movement', and it gives a good summary:

1. All is One—sometimes called 'consciousness' where there is no actual distinction between the material world and persons—a 'oneness of the universe.'
2. All is God—A pantheistic belief where we all blend into cosmic unity and there is not a God, but we are all gods and everything is god.
3. You are God—not individually as such, but part of humanity we are god, therefore god is in you and god is you.
4. The Need for Corrected Awareness—a "new consciousness" is needed in order to understand all of the above and to see the world in a different way, logic aside.
5. All religions are one—No one religion has all the answers to life and meaning. Jesus is just one of the many *guides*.
6. Things are progressing positively—The New Age provides a positive answer for those who are concerned about the future. Unlike Christianity with its 'prophets of doom' the New Age is *calling us to hope*.[20]

After decades of the New Age saturation in the West, the longings of people today have become even more desperate. McGrath writes that the New Age movement was 'responding to the void created by a secular humanism which has run out of steam'.[21]

Our culture today is filled with symbols and practices of the New Age, from crystals and dream catchers to holistic medicines and practices targeting mind, body, and spirit. Yoga and meditation, Mother Earth beliefs, tarot cards, beads, psychics, star signs, music, art and much more are readily sought. All is accepted, even if one sees it as kooky. There is no offence as all is embraced. In fact, the highest offence is to presume that there is only one exclusive truth.

The New Age glorifies self and permeates the West so completely that even Christians have unwittingly adopted aspects of its world view, which I discuss in following chapters.

The Human Potential Movement

Another movement that became popular in the '60s and '70s was the human potential movement (HPM). It emerged from humanistic therapy that flourished in the '40s and '50s.[22] Humanistic therapy theorists consisted of a group of psychologists, including Aldous Huxley and Abraham Maslow (whom many would know from Maslow's hierarchy of needs pyramid). At the top of the pyramid is self-actualisation, which is defined as achieving one's full potential including creative activities.[23]

Maslow published a book in 1964 titled *Religion, Values, and Peak Experience*. This set the stage for his belief that every human has the potential to have a transcendent experience without religion. Therefore, the top of Maslow's pyramid could be anything one might aspire to or follow as their own path, from Christ consciousness to Buddha consciousness. The premise was that when more people are born higher on the pyramid, then this, in turn, would make the world more peaceful and more equal.[24]

The second need on the pyramid is esteem needs, and it was from these ideas and theories that the self-esteem movement ideas originated. I'll discuss the self-esteem movement in the next chapter and how it helped produce a generation of unhappy, entitled, me-centred millennials, although Doctor Spock was doing a good job already with the baby boomers. (I discuss Dr. Spock and his child training ideas in a later chapter.)

A major aspect of the human potential movement was its teachings on the mind's ability to physically control the body. For example, deep meditation was proved to dramatically change brain waves, blood pressure, heart rate, and skin temperature.[25] A Harvard cardiologist, Herbert Benson, MD, began to study Tibetan monks and TM meditation and found it to be profoundly healing. It inspired him to help launch the field of mind-body medicine.[26]

It's interesting to compare the contribution of science, invention, medicine, education, literacy, visual arts, and other areas that Christian monks gave the world, as opposed to what the Eastern religious monks contributed.

According to the aforementioned Rabi R. Maharaj, he was taught to completely empty his mind and become one with the universe, and this was his main activity each day. Little else was achieved when totally focused inward in a meditative state. No matter how strong, brave, or intellectually gifted a man could be, it would be difficult to contribute to the good of society or to lift people from poverty while continually focused inward on oneness with the universe and seeking the true self. The significant difference was that the Christian monks focused outward on the Creator whereas the Hindu focused on the creature or self.

Regarding HPM, the Esalen Institute in California was established as a retreat centre for humanistic alternative education. Over the years it has been host to searching hippies, Timothy Leary and his types as well as scores of celebrities and other prominent people - and not just Americans. Esalen, as it is called for short, played a major role in the Human Potential Movement in the '60s and '70s and is still thriving today. Mike Murphy, one of the founders of Esalen explains that they wanted to 'be a center where we could explore conceptually the ideas that we were interested in. Namely that the cosmos, the universe itself, the whole evolutionary unfoldment is what a lot of philosophers call slumbering spirit. The divine is incarnate in the world and is present in us and is trying to manifest.'[27]

Paglia writes in her paper 'Cults and Cosmic Consciousness: Religious Vision in America in the 1960s' that Christian conservatives regularly, and probably with some justice, attack the self-actualisation or human potential school of psychology for its 'pagan' stress on personal needs and desires at the expense of moral reasoning and responsibility. For many people, humanistic psychology has indeed become a substitute for religion.[28]

Maslow also wrote a book titled *The Farther Reaches of Human Nature*, which had a significant influence on many during the '60s cultural revolution, including Betty Friedan, a major leader in the women's movement. Sue Ellen Browder, author of *Subverted: How I helped the Sexual Revolution Hijack the Women's Movement*, records the influence of Maslow's humanistic ideology on her as a young writer in the '60s searching for purpose. She explains its underpinnings:

> Maslow's humanistic theories contain strong elements of Christianity—but placed hope and trust in man's achievements (not in Christ) at the center of one's faith. In Maslow's worldview, the glorified human "self"—not God—was in charge of the universe. Dr. Paul Vitz, professor emeritus of psychology at New York University, has dubbed the religious sounding psychology Maslow and others developed in the 1960s and 1970s "the cult of self worship" or "selfism."[29]

Browder writes that Maslow's ideas were popular amongst people who thought themselves to be broad-minded, enlightened seekers. She was able to put Christ at the perimeters of her faith and not at the centre since he may require of her something more than what she was willing to give. She could confidently call herself a good person, and even Christian, and yet still live life the way she comfortably chose.

> Self-actualizing people, as Maslow described them, had many admirable traits I longed to possess and express. They were sensitive to beauty, detached from petty

socializing, and had a good natured (rather than cruel) sense of humor and were kind, caring ... Self-actualizers were also frequently capable of having a 'peak experience' (which Maslow described as 'a moment so wonderful it made you weep or get cold shivers of ecstasy'). Maslow placed the peak experience (not worship of God) at the heart of organized religion.[30]

Unwittingly, many Christians are seeking *a peak experience* when they attend a church service or worship, although they may not recognise it as such. To seek this only is skirting dangerously close to what professor of psychology Dr Paul Vitze describes as 'selfism'.[31] Watchman Nee would have described it as soulish.[32]

Tracing these steps back to where, why and how the baby boomer generation drifted away from their religious traditions and foundations of society is helpful in understanding how they failed to pass them on to the next generation, both through parenting and education. Helen Andrews, who researched and wrote about the baby boomer generation, said this:

> I always had a feeling that the millennial generation, my generation was a disinherited generation in some spiritual sense. That is, that the patrimony of our great American civilization just didn't get handed on to us the way it got handed on to previous generations. Functioning families, functioning churches, functioning schools, all of these seem like basic bare minimums that we just didn't get. Those were not handed off to us.[33]

As you can see, the loss that millennials feel is real, and this felt pain is a driving factor that causes many of them to look back for stability and direction.

Church, we must be ready to receive them. If we are just a friendly group that meets on Sundays and not a distinct biblical counter-culture displaying purity, selflessness, and brotherly love, we will miss them.

---

1. Paglia, "Cosmic Consciousness," 58.
2. Eskridge, "Jesus People."
3. Britannica, T. Editors of Encyclopaedia, "hippie," *Encyclopedia Britannica*, July 30, 2021, https://www.britannica.com/topic/hippie.
4. Paglia, "Cosmic Consciousness."
5. Ibid.
6. Ibid.
7. Paul Mason, *Maharishi Mahesh Yogi: The Biography of the Man Who Gave Transcendental Meditation to the World* (United Kingdom: Premanand, 2020).
8. Emma Seppälä, "20 Scientific Reasons to Start Meditating Today," *Psychology Today*, September 11, 2013, https://www.psychologytoday.com/au/blog/feeling-it/201309/20-scientific-reasons-start-meditating-today.
9. Dave Hunt and Rabi Maharaj, *Death of a Guru* (Fort Washington, Pennsylvania: Harvest House Publishers, 1984), 1030.
10. Ibid.
11. Ibid.
12. Julia Wick, "Aldous Huxley's Influence on the Esalen Institute," Longreads, accessed May 7, 2022, https://longreads.com/2015/06/09/aldous-huxleys-influence-on-the-esalen-institute.
13. Joe Carter, "9 Things You Should Know About the Rajneeshees," The Gospel Coalition, April 3, 2018, https://www.thegospelcoalition.org/article/9-things-know-rajneeshees.
14. Camille Paglia, "Cosmic Consciousness."
15. Ibid.
16. Ibid., 47.
17. Ibid., 48.
18. Ibid., 58.
19. David Holloway, "Yippies," Encyclopedia.com, accessed February 2, 2022, https://www.encyclopedia.com/media/encyclopedias-almanacs-transcripts-and-maps/yippies.
20. Gavin McGrath, "The Significance of the New Age Movement," *Churchman*, 105, no. 1 (1991): 30.
21. Ibid.
22. "Human-Potential Movement," the Free Dictionary, accessed January 13, 2020, https://medical-dictionary.thefreedictionary.com/Human-Potential+Movement.
23. "Maslow's Hierarchy of Needs," edraw, PDF, accessed April 4, 2022, https://www.edrawsoft.com/templates/pdf/needs-pyramid-chart.pdf.

24. Stephen Kiesling, "What Is the Human Potential Movement?" Spirituality & Health, accessed May 7, 2022, https://spiritualityhealth.com/articles/2020/09/25/the-human-potential-movement.

25. Ibid.

26. Ibid.

27. Kera Abraham and Mark C. Anderson, "One Half-Century and Esalen Institute," *Monterey Country Weekly*, last updated May 16, 2013, https://www.montereycountyweekly.com/news/cover/one-half-century-at-esalen-institute/article_97f3e295-a992-523c-90ea-9c082d56ebda.html.

28. Paglia, "Cosmic Consciousness."

29. Browder, 82–83.

30. Ibid., 83.

31. Ibid.

32. Watchman Nee, *The Latent Power of the Soul*, translated by Stephen Kaung (North Chesterfield, VA: Christian Fellowship Publishers, 1972).

33. Allie Beth Stuckie, "Blaming Boomers for Millennial's Problems | Guest Helen Andrews | Ep 446," accessed May 7, 2022, YouTube video, 47:10, https://www.youtube.com/watch?v=xZc6UHc54KE&t=449s.

— 7 —

The Self Movements

The mass rejection of the Christian faith in the '60s and '70s by the counter-culture movement created a void. Since the young boomers had rejected God, they, like every living soul, needed to find answers about purpose and meaning. They began to explore and embrace other philosophies that encouraged them to look within themselves to find those answers. In addition, they needed instructions to guide them along the way to reach their 'human potential'.

Hence the self-help and the self-esteem movements took off alongside the New Age movement and occult beliefs and practices that put self at the centre. These 'self' movements have expanded and developed since the '60s to what we have now—the open acceptance and uncritical embrace of every popular trending thought.

This chapter looks at the origins and philosophies behind some of these movements. As you read, you'll recognise trends that surfaced over the decades, be able to put them in perspective, and recognise the subtle deceptions of hollow philosophies that many of us might have embraced.

The Self-Esteem Movement

This movement or craze took off in the 1990s, but the ideas behind it were brewing since the '60s and '70s.[1] The following is only a brief overview; however, I believe it will strike a chord of familiarity with many readers because the self-esteem ideas were readily absorbed across the Western world and are still very much alive today.

The idea of teaching children self-esteem was first introduced to the Californian educational system in the 1990s by the Californian State Legislature, championed by a Democrat politician by the name of John Vasconcellos. Vasconcellos entered politics as a young man during the '60s cultural revolution and stayed until his retirement in 2004.[2] In politics, he was known for his non-conformity and described as 'colorful, witty, brilliant, angry, intellectual and elegantly foul of mouth'.[3] He was into self-improvement techniques and obscure forms of therapy, including those of the New Age Esalen Institute, which I briefly mentioned in the previous chapter.[4]

Vasconcellos led the charge to have self-esteem taught in Californian schools, the rationale being that 'low self-esteem was at the root of crime, drug addiction, teen pregnancy, and other problems'.[5] The premise was that if the self-esteem of children could be raised, then this would mean better educational performance and better life outcomes overall.

In the article 'The Decline of Traditional Honor in the West in the 20th Century', authors Brett and Kate McKay provide some more insight:

> In 1969, psychologist Nathaniel Brandon published a very influential paper called "The Psychology of Self-Esteem" in which he argued that "feelings of self-esteem are the key to success in life." Brandon's ideas were first institutionalized when a task force, charged by the California state legislature, formulated a set of recommendations entitled, "Toward a State of Esteem." The report argued that the low self-esteem caused a variety of ills ranging from academic failure to teen

> pregnancy and that teaching self-esteem in schools would be a "social vaccine" to inoculate kids from these problems. It recommended that every school district in California strive for "the promotion of self-esteem ... as a clearly stated goal, integrated into its total curriculum and informing all of its policies and operations" and that "course work in self-esteem should be required for credentials ... for all educators."[6]

Since low self-esteem was supposedly the cause of criminal behaviour, Vasconcellos claimed boosting children's self-esteem would reduce the burden on the criminal justice system and ultimately reduce crime and save the state finances. This financial benefit appealed to the conservatives as well and therefore had bipartisan support.

However, the self-esteem theory was later debunked categorically by empirical evidence. In fact, it was found that the opposite was true.[7] Many criminals are found to have an astoundingly high sense of self-esteem and illusions of superiority.[8] Good performance and achievement actually *build* self-esteem rather than self-esteem being the cause of good performance. Or to put it another way, poor achievement causes low self-esteem. This is the idea behind military training, where the high achievement demanded builds confidence and self-esteem in soldiers.

Brett & Kate McKay, in their article 'The Decline of Traditional Honor in the West in the 20th Century', wrote:

> Feeling good and true self-esteem, naturally follow from doing well. You can't pump kids full of self-esteem—it's something they have to earn for themselves, through true merit.[9]

One of the key outcomes of this philosophy was the elimination of competition from the classroom because it might cause hurt feelings and be harmful to a poor performer's esteem. Nowadays, everyone gets an award, even a 'participation trophy'. And of course, kids can see through this charade.

Nevertheless, Vasconcellos's brave new promise went ahead, and the teaching of self-esteem into the Californian education system was adopted wholeheartedly. It was also swept up by many other states across the nation. The craze hit schools hard, with various kinds of classroom interventions and exercises designed to make children feel good about themselves. Schools even stopped the use of red pens for correcting with the belief that red ink could harm a child's self-esteem. Around the school and in classrooms, posters and eye-catching messages plastered walls and mirrors telling children that they were the most special people in the world. High school yearbooks were required to show a picture of each student an equal number of times and awards ceremonies became much longer.

Steve Salerno, in his book *Sham: How the Self-Help Movement Made America Helpless*, states that 'rather than hiring better teachers and spending more money on actual schools and instruction, it became a surrogate for the stuff that might actually have done some good'.[10] Salerno gives more perspective on the origins of the destructive self-esteem ideas:

> Self-esteem-based education comes straight out of the theory of victimization, which was advanced in such early books as *I'm OK – You're OK*, and despite the titular message, the real point of the message was you're not okay, you're all broken inside and need to be fixed.[11]

But let me make it clear that despite the value of achievement, our true self esteem will never be fed by it. It should come from our creator, not our accomplishments or looks or social status. We all have intrinsic value regardless of where we measure on the world's success scale, and children have value and should know it because of their identity in God, their divine design, and their God-given destiny.

Critics of the self-esteem movement, such as Charles Krauthammer and 'Dr. Laura' Schlessinger, saw the self-esteem movement as yet another manifestation of the saccharine, mushy, self-help drivel that they said was undermining America.[12]

Jean Twenge, a psychologist and author, unwittingly sums up the effects of the self-esteem movement in the title of her book *Generation Me: Why Today's Young Americans are More Confident, Assertive, Entitled—and More Miserable Than Ever Before*. Twenge published a subsequent book titled *The Narcissism Epidemic*. She believes the self-obsession of today's generation is leaving them 'depressed, lonely and buried under piles of debt'.[13] And this is the fruit of individualism or selfism.

There is so much more to this topic, which makes some very interesting reading; however, the bottom line is that the self-esteem gospel *transformed* education in many parts of America and the West. Teachers and parents were encouraged *to avoid making kids feel bad* or they'd perform poorly. In addition, it was the hope that the teaching of self-esteem would close the achievement gap and promote *equity*. But the self-esteem experiment failed because it was simply another hollow philosophy made up by man.

The Self-Help Movement

The '60s and '70s were the age of the guru, yoga, meditation, mind, body, and spirit. There was so much to learn in order to reach the tip of the pyramid to self-actualisation, to reach our human potential. Many were still struggling with the penultimate esteem step on Maslow's pyramid. As our Western enlightened culture turned away from the transcendent to look inward, we became all about self.[14]

Today the self-help or self-improvement industry is so prolific that it is estimated to be worth approximately $10 billion.[15]

> The self-improvement market is wide and encompasses a large variety of products and services which range from books to e-books, online courses, coaching programs, webinars, … mobile apps etc.[16]

The world has lacked a spiritual replacement for our young people over the decades. In Paglia's view, the universities failed to address the spiritual cravings of the post-'60s period.[17] She describes the '60s and '70s as a time of spiritual crisis, with mainline religions split between their liberal and conservative sides, and the secular academic elite, along with celebrities, disrespecting the religious. Paglia describes these 'elites' as 'a mass of neo-pagan cults and superstitions seething beneath the surface'.[18]

Psychology and therapeutics became the replacement for the traditional Judeo-Christian faith of the West. The self-help and wellness gurus are now the ones we look to for answers, help, guidance, and comfort. Indeed, they seem to have the answers to life without demanding too much from us. The late Watchman Nee, a renowned Chinese evangelist and author, presented an interesting perspective on modern psychology way back in 1933:

> The field of psychology has undertaken unprecedented research in the modern age. What is psychology? The word itself is the combination of two Greek words: "psyche" which means soul and "logia" which means discourse. Hence psychology is "the science of the soul." The research engaged in by modern scientists is but a

> probing into the soul part of our being. It is limited to that part, the spirit not being touched."[19]

The spirit of man is left untouched and without a Shepherd when psychology neglects our Christian need of spiritual nurture.

As to self-help, the following were some books advertised by a major book distributor to start readers' purchases in 2021. The slick marketing declares: 'New Year, New You'. And there are lots of *gurus* to help us with *new knowledge* and techniques. Observe the titles of the books advertised:[20]

> *Not a Life Coach: Push Your Boundaries. Unlock Your Potential. Redefine Your Life*
>
> *Help Self: Learn from my mistakes so you can make different ones*
>
> *Un-cook Yourself: A Ratbag's Rules for Life*
>
> *Think Like a Monk: How to Train Your Mind for Peace and Purpose Everyday*
>
> *Darkness Is Golden: A Guide to Personal Transformation and Dealing with Life's Messiness*
>
> *Untamed: Stop Pleasing, Start Living*

All of these books and many more purport to provide the reader with a path forward to a better life, to gain control of one's future, to define and reach success, and to achieve peace.

Finally, what is known as the 'wellness syndrome' is prolific within our current culture. Steven Poole of the *Guardian* wrote a review of a book by that name that provides some great insight:

> Carl Cederstrom and Andre Spicer's brilliantly sardonic anatomy of this "wellness syndrome" concentrates on

The Self Movements

> the ways in which the pressure to be well operates as a moralising command and obliterates political engagement. The body, for adherents of wellness, becomes the only "truth system", and the withdrawal into it leads to "passive nihilism". If we are all obsessed with being well individually, the book warns, we will not be well together.[21]

Poole goes on to explain that:

> the authors' point out that the ideology of wellness shares with psychology's controversial "positive thinking" the twin assumptions that: you can be whatever you want to be; and therefore, b) if anything bad happens to you, it's no one's fault but your own.
>
> In this way, the apparent optimism of the public encouragement to "wellness" hides a brutal, libertarian lack of compassion.[22]

We have an aching spiritual void in our culture because the West has turned to face inward to self and satisfy what pleases self alone. People desperately need to find the way home, but the signposts have been removed. The church has the answer to those who are trapped in darkness and searching for light. We must return to biblical truth, deny self, and radically follow Jesus.

---

1. Jesse Singal, "How the Self-Esteem Craze Took Over America," The Cut, May, 2017, https://www.thecut.com/2017/05/self-esteem-grit-do-they-really-help.html.

2. Steve Chawkins, "John Vasconcellos dies at 82; father of California self-esteem panel," *Los Angeles Times*, May 25, 2014, https://www.latimes.com/local/obituaries/la-me-john-vasconcellos-20140526-story.html.

3. David E. Early, "Former California legislator John Vasconcellos, titan of the human-potential movement, dead at 82," *Mercury News*, last updated August 12, 2016, https://www.mercurynews.com/2014/05/24/former-california-legislator-john-vasconcellos-titan-of-the-human-potential-movement-dead-at-82.

4. Singal, "Self-Esteem Craze."

5. Chawkins, "John Vasconcellos dies."

6. Kate McKay, "Manly Honor VI: The Decline of Traditional Honor in the West in the 20th Century," The Art of Manliness, last updated June 4, 2021, https://www.artofmanliness.com/articles/manly-honor-vi-the-decline-of-traditional-honor-in-the-west-in-the-20th-century.

7. Singal, "Self-Esteem Craze."

8. "Prisoners have higher self-esteem than community members," *Metro World News*, January 13, 2014, https://www.metro.us/prisoners-have-higher-self-esteem-than-community-members.

9. McKay, "Manly Honor."

10. Singal, "Self-Esteem Craze."

11. Ibid.

12. Ibid.

13. Jean M. Twenge and W. Keith Campbell, *The Narcissism Epidemic* (New York: Atria, 2010).

14. A recent book traces the history of this phenomenon: Carl R. Trueman, *The Rise and Triumph of the Modern Self: Cultural Amnesia, Expressive Individualism, and the Road to Sexual Revolution* (Wheaton, Illinois: Crossway, 2020).

15. John LaRosa, "The $10 Billion Self-Improvement Market Adjusts to a New Generation," MarketResearch.com, October 11, 2018, https://blog.marketresearch.com/the-10-billion-self-improvement-market-adjusts-to-new-generation.

16. Iulia-Cristina Uță, "The Self-Improvement Industry Is Estimated to Grow to $13.2 billion by 2022," BRAND MINDS, June 27, 2019, https://brandminds.live/the-self-improvement-industry-is-estimated-to-grow-to-13-2-billion-by-2022.

17. Paglia, "Cosmic Consciousness."

18. Ibid.

19. Nee, "Latent Power."

20. Email received from Booktopia, "Achieve All Your Resolutions in 2021," sent January 15, 2021.

21. Steven Poole, "The Wellness Syndrome by Carl Cederström & André Spicer – exploitation with a smiley face," the *Guardian*, January 22, 2015, https://www.theguardian.com/books/2015/jan/22/the-wellness-syndrome-carl-cederstrom-andre-spicer-persuasive-diagnosis.

22. Ibid.

— 8 —

New Age Syncretism

Over the decades, many New Age beliefs, practices, and thinking were syncretised into Western Christian churches. That is, beliefs and ideas from outside scriptural teaching blended with Christian faith and practice. Syncretism aims to create unity because it allows for inclusion and acceptance of other beliefs and practices. The result is that Christianity then becomes less offensive, less exclusive, and more tolerable because it doesn't challenge the beliefs of the world.

This syncretism has weakened the Western Christian church and contributed to its decline, especially since the '60s and '70s when the door was flung open for the entrance of Eastern religious beliefs and practices. Compare that to the church in closed countries, where the outlawed Christian faith is strong and stands distinct as a counter-culture to the world around them. (This is discussed further in later chapters.) The church in the West must be a distinct counter-culture to grow, that is to have strong marriages, strong families, strong churches, strong communities, strong leaders, and strong and spiritually healthy people of God.

False teaching was a significant problem of the early church. The writers of the New Testament were continually addressing empty philosophies and false teaching that had crept in and deceived many. How much more susceptible is the church today to false teaching because of the sophistication of mass communication and world travel, where we are constantly exposed to many more ideas? And these ideas and philosophies are very attractive and often sound Christian.

The purpose of this chapter is to expose some of the syncretism that we commonly see today. If this can open our eyes and we can see the harm it's doing to our witness and spiritual authority, then we might repent, return to our first love, hold on to what we have, and follow Jesus—our true Saviour and King.

To illustrate a common practice that has crept in amongst many Christians in the West, I begin with New Thought and a story.

The New Thought Movement

'Is it okay to envision something into reality? Like, envision something and ask God to give it to me and speak it into existence?' A young Christian friend asked me this question. She had been pondering a certain practice and teaching in her church. A mature Christian leader challenged her to envision the home she wanted to build and begin speaking it into existence through prayer. Something didn't seem right about this, but everyone in her church seemed so passionate in their Christian faith and always so positive. My young friend's uneasiness with this was well founded.

New Thought significantly influences Christianity in the West, although many would not recognise it by that name. It's believed to have originated back in the 1800s by American Phineas Quimby, who founded what is called a religio-metaphysical healing cult. Quimby was a mentalist and mesmerist who discovered that he could heal by suggestion.[1] Mary Baker Eddy, the founder of Christian Science, was a disciple of Quimby.

New Thought is couched in very Christianised terms and is easily mistaken as Christian doctrine. Even Quimby believed

New Age Syncretism

that he rediscovered the healing methods of Jesus.[2] Many New Thought teachers and advocates today use Scripture to back up their beliefs.

New Thought focuses more on the mind. A person has divine power to create their 'right' reality using their thoughts. New Thought teacher Dr. Michelle Medrano has a video that provides a good overview of these ideas. She says that New Thought is the phrase that hangs like an umbrella over a number of spiritual traditions that exist in the world today, therefore she sees New Thought as the umbrella phrase for unity. The teaching is called the science of mind and spirit. Divine science, and even some field of Christian Science, can fit New Thought beliefs. But Medrano emphasises that it's all about traditions because she says that what New Thought teaches isn't really new; it's ancient, and the concepts are woven through many traditions from many different parts of the world. She explains that New Thought is the unique contribution that the United States has made to the formation of religion in our world. In essence, the belief system teaches people to think new thoughts.[3]

And the new thoughts are all positive thoughts. Negative thoughts are looked down upon because all new thoughts need to be about love and peace and positive things. Words and concepts such as wrath and judgement have no place in New Thought. Therefore, with the Jesus of New Thought, all are saved, there is a second chance, all paths lead to God, and there is acceptance of all beliefs. This is what is called universalism.[4]

The idea of 'Christ consciousness' is one of the teachings of New Thought. The following is part of an explanation from the Mystical Church of Christ that helps those wishing to live 'a Christ-centred spiritual life':

> The Christ is an aspect that exists in a mostly dormant state in each human being. It is the very pure God Self that exists in each person, waiting be reached, discovered and crowned as the ruler of our being. Our task is to take on the Christ and this is done deliberately through patient inner work.[5]

New Thought and New Age both advocate love, a utopian-type mentality, total peace, no anger, no bitterness, no negativity, and no confrontation or disagreements. Negativity, including conflict, is equivalent to sin. New Thought ideas have been embraced by many Christians unwittingly, and this is what my young friend experienced in her church—speaking things into existence with the God-power we have within us.

Young People and New Thought

New Thought has not just crept into churches; it is also a growing movement, and young people seem to be embracing it, more so in recent years. A recent *New York Times* article in 2021 is titled 'Manifesting for the Rest of Us—A new generation has turned to an aeons-old practice of envisioning positive outcomes'.[6] Young people are turning to positive thinking to achieve material and psychic rewards *through sheer force of mind*. Manifesting is, as the title of the article states, 'envisioning positive outcomes'. It goes on:

> Manifesting sits alongside a smattering of belief systems—astrology, tarot, paganism and their metaphysical cousins—being resurrected by a youthful generation in the name of wellness. "For Gen Z in particular- it can be a form of self soothing," said Lucie Greene, a writer and trend forecaster in New York. "It's a way to make sense of things in a moment where nothing makes sense."

> It is especially meaningful, Miss Greene went on, to those tribes of teenagers and people in their early 20s whose hopes have been flattened or derailed by a pandemic-imposed social and economic malaise. In such a fraught climate, she said "it's cathartic to feel you have some control over your destiny."

We all need to feel we can have some control over our destiny in this crazy world, and this gives people that illusion.

The article goes on to explain that this isn't just a fad but a coping mechanism—a legitimate alternative that organised religion or psychotherapy may not always provide.

'Manifesting' is a modern concept of what is known as the law of attraction, popularised in Rhonda Byrne's best-selling wellness book titled *The Secret*, released in 2005 and updated in 2020 as *The Greatest Secret*, which is wildly popular with adults of all ages. It has been syncretised into Christian domains, particularly the Word of Faith movement (a biblical movement which believes that words can be used to manipulate the faith-force and thus create what they believe Scripture promises of health and wealth).[7] Underlying this concept is seeking to use spirituality for self-purposes. As US theologian Albert Mohler says, 'It makes God into a great source of energy at our disposal.'[8]

The power of positive thinking and manifesting has been rebranded as 'wellness', and this is part of the self-help movement.

My young friend was right to feel uncomfortable about visualising and speaking something into existence through prayer. The prayer part is just the Christian term added to the old practice of 'manifesting'.

Oneness and Other Things

Melissa Doherty, co-author of the book *From New Age to Christianity* outlines five influences that I believe provide a good basic overview of how New Age beliefs have crept into churches today or just embraced by Christians.[9] Notice in the following summary how each one builds upon the other and is interconnected:

1. **The Law of Attraction**: this is the ability to attract into our lives whatever we are focusing on.[10] To put it simply, like attracts like. It is a pseudo-science that suggests that what you think can be your reality because of the vibrations and energy that come from our thoughts. All thoughts will eventually materialise; so one must concentrate on positive confession. The highest thought is love. If you are on this vibration, you will always get what you want. You will recognise this is from New Thought teaching, but it goes right back to Buddhism and the concept of what we might know as karma. Speaking things into existence, name it and claim it, and so on have their origins in New Thought.

2. **Oneness**: This is about unity. There are many definitions of oneness, like this:

   > Oneness is a state of non division. Perception of reality as one consciousness, one Being. That place where Divine is All that there is. Experiencing life in this state of oneness is one of bliss, ecstasy and wholeness.[11]

   The oneness concept has been syncretised into Christianity through terms like peace, harmony, love, no fear, we are all one/all equal/all in this together. Therefore, we allow all beliefs in the door as we want to be loving and tolerant. If there is objection, then it's a sign of intolerance, being unloving, judgementalism, and, dare I say, even 'hate'. Doherty believes that *we sacrifice good theology on the altar of unity.*

3. **Religious pluralism**: The belief that all paths lead to God and that Jesus is *a* way but not *the* way to God. Pluralism is like syncretism in that churches might adopt new ideas to win the unbeliever. It creates a hybrid type of belief. Oneness and pluralism build upon each other and are both strong elements of progressive Christianity. Regarding progressive Christianity, many young people are embracing these beliefs to the detriment of the gospel. There is much harmony with these progressive beliefs and the current secular narratives, particularly social justice and wokism. (For a good explanation of progressive Christianity, I recommend Alisa Childers book, *Another Gospel? A Lifelong Christian Seeks Truth in Response to Progressive Christianity* (2021).[12]

4. **Universalism**: is the fourth characteristic, a doctrine that espouses that all people will be saved and go to heaven. There is no wrath, no justice, no judgement. In the end, it is all love. Again, this is a predominant teaching of progressive Christianity. The term 'universal reconciliation' is how it has been presented in Christianity.

5. **Mysticism**: Dougherty emphasises that not all Christian mysticism is New Age. By mysticism, she states that it is 'purposefully seeking a spiritual experience … for the purpose of power, hidden knowledge, hidden truth, extra biblical knowledge, manifestations of glory, powerful spiritual experiences…'[13] It's when experience becomes one's truth; if you want to know God, then

you need to have a powerful spiritual experience with him. This relates with the self-actualisation peak of Maslow's hierarchy of needs. Experience usurps Scripture. 'The more mindless, the more spiritual you'll become'.[14]

Perennialism

Perennialism is another philosophy gaining popularity, with both Western culture and the Christian faith absorbing it. According to *The Spiritual Life* website:

> The **Perennial philosophy**, also referred to as **perennialism** and **perennial wisdom**, is a perspective in spirituality that views all of the world's religious traditions as sharing a single, metaphysical truth or origin from which all esoteric and exoteric knowledge and doctrine has grown.[15]

Perennialism is like universalism but not the same. Where universalism was more of a response to the exclusiveness of Christian doctrine about only one way to salvation, perennialism, on the other hand, seeks to bring all religions and beliefs together by claiming that every culture and faith has their own expression or 'tradition' that leads to the one truth. So even though on the outside (exoteric) all religions look different, on the inside (esoteric), they are the same and lead to God.

> Followers of Perennial Wisdom do not, however, advocate a global faith or a uniting of all religions. They believe that the same thread of wisdom runs through all religions, and therefore, all religions share and eventually lead to the same core truth and Divine Reality. Consequently, all could find the Perennial truths via their own faith tradition through an inward journey

(mysticism). The inner journey via mystical practices is the bridge that leads one to the truth that unites these religions.[16]

Many of us have not recognised the influence of perennial philosophy in our culture, and even our Christian faith, because we assume we share the same language. For example, if someone said they follow the 'Christian tradition' or 'Christian wisdom tradition', then the older generations might interpret that as another way—even a politically correct version—of professing to be a Christian. New Thought is a good example of using perennial language to describe the Christian faith—'it's ancient and the concepts are woven through many traditions from many different parts of our world'.[17]

There are other subtle aspects of perennial philosophy that we now see amongst Christians. Marcia Montenegro names a number of them: the Contemplative Aspect, Panentheism, Greater Knowing, the Greater Self, Justice, and the True Self as well as the teaching on the Enneagram. In her research and writing she explains, 'the Enneagram purports to lead a person to not only self-understanding, but to an integration of all aspects of the self and, ultimately, to an awakening to the true Self. 'Self' is capitalised because the Self is considered by the original (and most contemporary) Enneagram teachers to be divine.'[18]

Since mystical practices in perennial wisdom lead to the one truth, perennialism strongly advocates contemplative techniques. Montenegro, in her article 'Perennial Wisdom and Christianity: Compatible?', explains:

> The term contemplative in this context refers to advocating certain practices that involve techniques such as following one's breath, repeating a word or words, imaginative prayer, and/or other techniques designed to

bring one into a state of (non-thinking) awareness of the Divine and union with the Divine. This may go under the names prayer, meditation, centering, contemplative prayer, or other terms.[19]

Spiritual mystical practices are becoming widespread amongst Christians today, therefore discernment is essential, and discernment is difficult without solid biblical literacy.

The Pagan Cult of Gaia

The environmental movement was birthed in the '60s and '70s, which I discuss in a later chapter. However, it is important to briefly mention the spiritual aspect of environmentalism that has become prominent today, often referred to as the 'green religion'.

Michael Shellenberger, an award-winning environmental scientist, wrote in his book *Apocalypse Never: Why Environmental Alarmism Hurts Us All* the following critique about the religion of environmentalism:

> Environmentalism today is the dominant secular religion of the educated upper-middle-class elite in most developed and many developing nations. It provides a new story about our collective and individual purpose. It designates good guys and bad guys, heroes and villains. And it does so in the language of science, which provides it with legitimacy.
>
> On the one hand, environmentalism and its sister religion, vegetarianism, appear to be a radical break from the Judeo-Christian religious tradition. For starters, environmentalists themselves do not tend to be believers or strong believers, in Judeo-Christianity. In particular, environmentalists reject the view that

humans have, or should have, dominion, or control, over Earth.[20]

Stellenberger further explains that environmentalism replaces God with nature, and human problems result when we don't adjust ourselves to nature. He believes priests and preachers have been replaced by scientists. Stellenberger quotes young Greta Thunberg, 'I want you to listen to the scientists!'[21] (exclamation mine).

On the Sunday before the United Nations Conference on Environment and Development (UNCED) many religious leaders met and issued a one-page declaration that included the following statements:

- The ecological crisis is a symptom of the spiritual crisis of the human being, resulting from ignorance.

- We must therefore transform our attitudes and values, and adopt a renewed respect for the superior law of Divine Nature.

- Individuals and governments need to evolve 'Earth Ethics' with a deeply spiritual orientation or the earth will cleanse itself of all destructive force.

- We believe that the universe is sacred because all is one.[22]

The 'all is one' idea again belies the New Age pagan underpinnings of environmentalism. And the Gaia hypothesis provides a scientific substance to support the Gaia religion. It also supports the idea of monism, the belief that all is one and we are all connected, as well as the New Age philosophy of perennialism. Phrases like 'earth ethics' presuppose moral and religious roots that motivate concern for Mother Earth. They rightly recognise the spiritual crises of mankind; however, the solution they offer will not save our souls.

Christian young people urgently need a biblical world view on the environment (or creation) as many unwittingly absorb the philosophy of environmentalism. Chapter 11 provides a biblical world view on this issue that offers much more hope than what is expounded through the green religion.

The Cult of the Self

This chapter provided only a brief snapshot of a few prevalent New Age ideas and practices that Christians embrace, particularly young people. All of these ideas and beliefs—New Thought, perennialism, oneness, and environmentalism—sound positive, caring, and just. They address our deeply felt needs of unity, hope, and love. In addition, they appease our sinful nature by allowing us to form our own morality and truth, even convincing us of our oneness with the divine within. And these new ideas glorify self and turn us inward—to the point that we are, unwittingly, in rebellion against God. Michael Stafford eloquently explains the cult of the self thus:

> The Cult of the Self also misdirects human desire away from God and toward a never-ending series of illusions for us to chase ... According to the Bible, the ancient Israelites often strayed from worship of God into idolatry. Today, America has done the same - except, rather than placing a golden calf upon an altar, we have erected a mirror. And in that mirror, we give glory to our own reflections. At its core, this Cult of the Self is an act of rebellion against all external authority over the individual - including, ultimately, God's. Before we make a desert of our life, or of our world, we must first have a desert inside us. The Cult of the Self is the force

driving the process of desertification in modernity - it creates internal, and then external, wastelands.

The Cult of the Self is based on a mistaken anthropology, a false understanding of the nature of the human person. As a result, it advances a disordered form of extreme individualism that understands liberty to be synonymous with personal license. It is relativistic and nihilistic; materialist and utilitarian. Autonomy - choice - is its highest, and perhaps only, value.[23]

Any teaching that directs our desire away from God needs to be seriously examined. We must throw off our foreign practices and ideas, deny self, and radically follow Jesus.

> *'For the flesh desires what is contrary to the Spirit, and the Spirit what is contrary to the flesh. They are in conflict with each other, so that you are not to do whatever you want'*
> *(Galatians 5:17).*

---

1. Britannica, T. Editors of Encyclopaedia, "Phineas Parkhurst Quimby," *Britannica*, accessed May 7, 2022, https://www.britannica.com/biography/Phineas-Parkhurst-Quimby.

2. Ibid.

3. Mile Hi Church, "NEW THOUGHT MOVEMENT in a NUTSHELL - Contemplate This with Dr. Michelle Medrano - Episode 1," uploaded January 22, 2018, YouTube video, 3:07, https://www.youtube.com/watch?v=28u-Szb-AGk.

4. Alisa Childers, "Is your church teaching New Age Ideas? With Melissa Dougherty," uploaded December 6, 2020, YouTube video, 59:53, https://www.youtube.com/watch?v=_nKrJvOdl3w.

5. "What is Christ Consciousness," The Mystical Church of Christ, August 22, 2018, https://www.mysticalchurchofchrist.org/2018/08/22/christ-consciousness.

6. Ruth La Ferla, "Manifesting, for the Rest of Us," *New York Times*, January 23, 2021, https://www.nytimes.com/2021/01/20/style/self-care/how-to-manifest-2021.html.

7. "Is the Word of Faith movement biblical?" GotQuestions.org, accessed June 21, 2021, https://www.gotquestions.org/Word-Faith.html.
8. "The Briefing," Albert Mohler, podcast, 22:05, January 29, 2021, https://albertmohler.com/2021/01/29/briefing-1-29-21.
9. Dougherty, "church teaching New Age?"
10. "What Is The Law Of Attraction? Open Your Eyes To A World Of Endless Possibilities," The Law of Attraction, accessed January 12, 2021, https://www.thelawofattraction.com/what-is-the-law-of-attraction.
11. Inelia Benz, "What is Oneness?" HiRa Hosèn, accessed January 12, 2021, https://www.tantraoftheheart.com/oneness.
12. You can buy her book from https://www.alisachilders.com/anothergospel.html.
13. Dougherty, "Is your church?"
14. Ibid.
15. "What Is Perennial Philosophy?" The Spiritual Life, accessed December 31, 2021, https://slife.org/perennial-philosophy.
16. Marcia Montenegro, "Perennial Wisdom and Christianity: Compatible?" Christian Answers for the New Age, accessed January 2, 2022, http://christiananswersforthenewage.org/Articles_Perennial%20Philosophy.aspx.
17. Medrano, "NEW THOUGHT MOVEMENT."
18. Marcia Montenegro, "The Enneagram GPS: Gnostic Path to Self," Christian Answers for the New Age, March 2011, http://www.christiananswersforthenewage.org/Articles_Enneagram.html
19. Montenegro, "Perennial Wisdom."
20. Michael Shellenberger, *Apocalypse Never: Why Environmental Alarmism Hurts Us All* (New York: HarperCollins Publishers, 2020), 263.
21. Ibid., 264.
22. Loren Wilkinson, "Gaia spirituality: a Christian critique," *themelios*, 18 no. 3, https://www.thegospelcoalition.org/themelios/article/gaia-spirituality-a-christian-critique.
23. Michael Stafford, "Christian resistance to the 'Cult of the Self'," *ABC Australia*, March 31, 2013, https://www.abc.net.au/religion/christian-resistance-to-the-cult-of-the-self/10099956.

— 9 —

The Sexual Revolution

Perhaps one of the most far-reaching impacts of the baby boomer revolt against religious traditions and civil institutions of their forefathers was the sexual revolution. It was a time when young people began to challenge the rules of conduct around sexual behaviour—particularly the traditional, accepted norm of heterosexual relations being only within the confines of marriage.

Again, more and more young people are looking around at the sexual confusion of today and are tracing back history to when things were stable and society had instructions and guidelines. One young man put it so well when he told me:

> A lot of young people who aren't religious, or with a Christian background, are beginning to notice all the insanity that is happening at the moment. And so they are waking up and saying, "Hold on, wait, what's going on now?" Things like, there are more than two genders, the environmental madness, how we need to reinvent society, how people don't want to work anymore, how the mainstream media is completely detached from reality, how everything is about racism, all the woke insanity ... even though they don't consider themselves spiritual or religious, they are realising and adopting a respect for Christianity. And maybe that's as far as it's going for now, but at least a respect for Christianity as the father of all these good things. All of these good

> things that they have been awoken to ... And they are starting to trace these back and seeing that they come from Christianity, most of them, and so they're developing a respect for that.

This is very encouraging, but again, the church must be ready. It must be distinct from the world and not the same.

For those who don't know what the word 'woke' means, it simply describes the state of being aware or awake to all the perceived prejudices and attitudes or power dynamics that exist in the structures of our society. Wokeness is based on the cultural Marxist world view.

There were significant external contributors to the sexual revolution of the 1960s, and that's what the first section of this chapter explores. In the next section, I will look at the changes in thinking that are driving the sexual revolution today. As limited as this chapter is in offering a sound overview of the sexual revolution (it would take volumes of books), my goal is for you to get some insight. Hopefully it will spark your curiosity to read further.

It Started with a Pill

Perhaps the major external contributor of the sexual revolution was the invention of the pill, which became available in 1961. Initially only for married women, in 1967, unmarried women were legally given access. For the first time in history, female baby boomers could now engage in casual sex just like men—without the fear of pregnancy. This was a huge win for them, but more on that later.

Linked to contraception availability, the rise of the pro-choice movement in the '60s also had an impact. Progressive women, along with their male sympathisers, joined forces to advocate for the legalisation of abortion. By the late 1960s, abortion was finally legalised in some form in sixteen American states. The final nail in the coffin for the unborn was the Roe vs. Wade ruling by the American Supreme Court in 1973, which legalised abortion nationally and created a precedent for other nations to follow. Women now had much more assurance of sexual freedom and choice if the first line of defence (contraception) failed.

Another less-known contributor that allowed for more sexual freedom was the invention of penicillin. Although discovered in 1928, penicillin couldn't be produced in large quantities until around 1941.[1] Used to treat syphilis, the mass production and growing availability in the '40s and '50s caused a huge decrease in the disease. The risk of contracting syphilis and dying a horrible death had been a deterrent to sexual promiscuity.

Interestingly, penicillin availability and the contraceptive pill led to a significant rise in sexually transmitted diseases and unwanted pregnancies.[2]

During the '60s and '70s, men's 'girlie' magazines were thriving. Millions of men across America, and soldiers stationed overseas, were buying popular titles. No doubt these magazines provided a service to soldiers on the field during the Vietnam and Korean War.

One of those 1950s' girlie mags was *Playboy*, founded by Hugh Hefner in 1953. The content of scantily dressed females was aimed at the male population between the ages of twenty-one and forty-five.[3] The erotic pictures of the '50s and '60s would probably be viewed as pretty low level today, but back then, Playboy Magazine became the world's most popular magazine: 'By the 1960s, *Playboy* was so huge that Hugh was able to move into the Playboy Mansion, which over the years became synonymous with a "playboy" lifestyle.'[4]

Today the girlie magazines have been superseded by free-for-all, virtual, online videos through multi-billion-dollar pornography websites.

In addition to the girlie magazines, women's magazines like *Cosmopolitan* supported the ideals of sexual revolution, influencing young women to pursue sex without strings as they pursued their corporate careers.

The '60s saw TV surpassing newspapers as an information source until it was estimated that around 90 percent of households in the USA had a TV.[5] It was the next step up in sophistication from the radio. Significantly, in 1968, the Motion Picture Production Code (Hays Code) that regulated the standards for the majority of US-produced motion pictures was abolished. Granted, it needed some serious overhaul; however, throwing it out for more subjective standards was not the best idea.

> The Sexual Revolution of the '60s meant audiences were more open to topics that had been previously thought of as vulgar. The Hays Code was officially replaced in 1968 by the Motion Picture Association of America's film rating system (MPAA), and it had four rating tiers: G for general exhibition (all ages), M for mature audiences (people over the age of 12), R for restricted (children under 16 must be accompanied by an adult), and X for extremely graphic (only people 18 or over will be admitted).[6]

Fast forward to 1981 and we see the outcomes of the easing of regulations with the introduction of MTV (Music Television) a twenty-four-hour platform for music videos and pop culture. The first song MTV played was one called 'Video Killed the Radio Star' from a band called the Buggles.[7] Ben Shapiro, in his 2005 book *Porn Generation: How Social Liberalism Is Corrupting*

Our Future, describes the effects MTV had on American kids. Referring to his generation at the time, he asks the question:

> Are kids truly 'smarter' because by age twelve, they describe themselves as "flirtatious, sexy, trendy, cool."? Or are they striving to imitate the "adult," "smart" behaviour modelled for them by pop culture? The loss of innocence and the rise of jadedness is a direct result of negligent parenting and immersion of children into an ever-deepening pool of pop culture materialism—a trend that MTV thrives on.[8]

One young man I interviewed for my previous book *Lost Boys*, who became addicted to pornography in his teens, told me that before he could access porn freely, he watched the raunchy videos on MTV instead. If you have the fortitude, take a look at some of the music videos our children and teens are consuming today and you'll get the picture.

At an event I attended, a man in his thirties—who grew up without a father in the home—told the audience that he learned to be a man and how to treat women from watching the raunchy, sexualised music videos on MTV in his youth. In particular, he learned that he needed to take a girl home after every party.

Another little-known aspect of the sexual revolution was the gay liberation movement. During the cultural revolution era, the practice of homosexuality was illegal, considered by general society a mental illness and perverse. In addition to the stigma and what that carried, homosexuals were persecuted for another reason we don't hear much about. During the Cold War, there was suspicion that citizens in sensitive government jobs were subject to blackmail and coercion by Soviet spies. Those practicing homosexuality were considered a risk for extortion and therefore some lost their jobs or were treated with distrust.[9]

THE NEXT REVOLUTION

This placed considerable pressure and stress on practicing homosexuals on top of the existing cultural stigmas.

It is important to note that the gay liberation movement was birthed in the late '60s and early '70s, and an event at Stonewall Inn triggered it:

> On June 28, 1969, New York City police raided the Stonewall Inn. It was a raid like so many others, but on this night the inn's patrons fought back by hurling rocks and bottles at the police. Over the next week two additional riots broke out in the neighborhood in protest.
>
> The uprisings ignited a new atmosphere of militant gay liberation. A new generation of activist organizations emerged, including the Gay Liberation Front and the Gay Activist Alliance. Like the homophile movement, these new organizations sought to end discrimination against gays and lesbians. Unlike the homophile organizations, however, these advocates for "gay liberation" embraced much more aggressive tactics throughout the 1970s.[10]

And this movement decades on led to the redefinition of the traditional institution of marriage by governments around the world. In the last decades, the state has replaced religion as the authority that defines marriage.

This has not come without a cost to our society. The legalisation of same-sex marriage enshrines in law that children can be raised without a biological mother or a biological father. Ethically, there is some debate over an adult's right to bear children and a child's right to be raised by their biological father and mother. Children have no voice in this debate, so it is never heard. In addition, since a same-sex couple cannot procreate naturally, it creates many more issues. One of those issues is commercial surrogacy, where wealthy same-sex couples pay women (many in poor nations) to carry and give birth to their children. If you haven't heard of this industry, just google 'commercial surrogacy' and read some of the research, particularly about the plight of women in India and why it was supposedly banned there in 2018. Babies now have become a commodity that can be bought and sold.

Finally, but no less important, was the women's liberation movement, as it was called in the '60s and '70s. This movement influenced the sexual revolution and was somewhat connected to other movements going on at the time, including the gay liberation movement. If you don't know the history of the feminist movement or the underlying ideology, then it would be worth your while to do some research on it.

The significant thing that transpired in 1967 was that the sexual revolution and the women's movement, each separate with different motivations and purposes, became united. (I discuss this in more detail in the next chapter.) Up until this time, the women's movement was not about sexual freedom and reproductive rights issues; it was primarily about equality in the workplace and education.

In 1967, when the US National Organisation for Women, under the leadership of Betty Friedan, embraced abortion, it split the movement. Scores of women parted ways because of the new, radical agenda. Many women of the movement did not agree with abortion or the anti-men and anti-family sentiment, nor with the sexual promiscuity promoted by the radical feminists. However, these radicals gradually gained the greatest influence. Sue Ellen Browder explains how the women's movement got 'hopelessly off track', saying it was the militant feminists of the '60s and '70s that gave birth to the third-wave feminism we see today.[11]

During this time, a new, radical group of feminists emerged, led by women such as Kate Millett, who wrote the book *Sexual Politics*—which was compulsory reading for the women's studies departments at universities and still is today. *Time* magazine dubbed Kate 'the Karl Marx of the women's movement' as her ideas were based on Marxist ideology of oppression.[12]

It was back in the 1960s that these radical ideologues mapped out a plan to 'destroy the patriarchy' through 'promoting promiscuity, eroticism, prostitution, and homosexuality'.[13] Therefore women engaging in free sexual expression outside marriage and biological norms were not only engaging in 'free love' but also fighting a cause for a greater purpose—to destroy the patriarchy; that is, ridding society of strong, monogamous men. Hence the destruction of two vital civic institutions of fatherhood and family we are witnessing today. Sadly, it appears that young women of the day who were caught up in fighting for the cause were unaware of the greater goal of the radical elite. I fear it is much the same today.

To further explain the point, as it is an important one: culturally, women have been considered the 'sexual gatekeepers' of society. (I unpack this later in the chapter.) Therefore, the sexual revolution needed to be tied to the women's movement. Go after the gatekeepers of sex and sexual 'freedom' could be attained. The pill and then abortion rights provided the means for women who wanted the same sexual freedom as men to have it—sexual freedom without the responsibility of pregnancy. The radical ideologues then pointed the way, convincing women of the lie that pursuing this would lead to *freedom*.

The New Sexual Revolution

The free love revolution of the '60s and '70s that sought to dismantle traditional sexual codes has gained momentum over the decades, having devastating effects on today's generation. Fifty years ago, the spread of pop culture was much slower and primarily distributed through pop music on the radio or in the old black record form. TV, with about three channels initially, was more focused on family viewing. Together with magazines, these were all much easier for parents and teachers to regulate. However, the effects of the disbandment of the standards code for film and TV and the gradual increase in explicit sexual content, including the introduction of MTV in the eighties, has meant that each generation has been more sexualised at a younger age than the previous.

Today, technology provides the most sophisticated and effective means to carry the sexual revolution narratives across the world in real time. With the release of the World Wide Web into the public domain in 1993, and its availability increasing each year since, communication has been revolutionised.

We are living in a new era that some call the 'techno sexual era'.[14]

In the modern 21st century, even little children are continually connected to the internet on mobile phones, which provides today's digital natives with instantaneous information, and entertainment. And, if needed, they have sexual gratification through voyeurism (the practice of obtaining satisfaction by observing others in sexual acts, the practice of taking pleasure in observing something private, sordid, or scandalous).[15] I wrote about this in my book *Lost Boys*:

> Our adversary has been using cyber warfare for decades. I believe one of his deadliest strategies is pornography. Its reach has been pervasive on men—old and young, married and single, fathers, grandfathers, brothers, sons, and even our little boys. It has even reached our girls. Every debauched, perverted, and vulgar sexual act one

> can imagine from any pit of darkness around the world is now accessible, affordable, anonymous, and aggressive toward little children. Kids are watching it on their phones in the playground and are consuming porn sometimes multiple times per day ... And this has been happening for years right under our noses ... Sadly, kids with unrestricted and unsupervised use of devices is having detrimental effects. Research by a security technology company found that 'one in 10 visitors of porn sites is under 10 years old'. Children are not just viewing what we would imagine as normal porn, they are consuming some of the most degrading and violent scenes imaginable, even live-streamed.[16]

The devastation of this pandemic upon the church has been unfathomable. By the time many of our boys enter manhood and marriage, many are already sexually broken.

The Ideas Driving Today's Sexual Revolution

Carl R. Trueman, in his book *The Rise and Triumph of the Modern Self: Cultural amnesia, expressive individualism and the road to Sexual Revolution*, provides a valuable and insightful perspective on the ideological thinking that has brought on the revolutionary changes of the ongoing sexual revolution, and I quote him at length here as he is very articulate.

> When I use the term sexual revolution, I am referring to the radical and ongoing transformation of sexual attitudes and behaviours that has occurred in the West since the early 1960s. Various factors have contributed to this shift, from the advent of the pill to the anonymity of the internet.
> The behaviours that characterise the sexual revolution

are not unprecedented: homosexuality, pornography and sex outside the bounds of marriage, for example, have been hardy perennials throughout human history. What marks the modern sexual revolution out as distinctive is the way it has normalised these and other sexual phenomena ... The sexual revolution does not simply represent a growth in the routine transgression of traditional sexual codes or even a modest expansion of the boundaries of what is and is not acceptable sexual behaviour; rather it involves the abolition of such codes in their entirety. More than that, it has come in certain areas, such as that of homosexuality, to require the positive repudiation of traditional sexual mores to the point where belief in, or maintenance of, such traditional views has come to be seen as ridiculous and even a sign of serious mental or moral deficiency.

The most obvious evidence of this change is the way language has been transformed to serve the purpose of rendering illegitimate any dissent from the current political consensus on sexuality. Criticism of homosexuality is now homophobia; that of transgenderism is transphobia. The use of the term phobia is deliberate and effectively places such criticism of the new sexual culture into the realm of the irrational and points toward an underlying bigotry on the part of those who hold such views. ...

... to be sexually inactive is to be a less-than-whole person, to be obviously unfulfilled or weird. The old sexual codes of celibacy outside marriage and chastity within it are considered, ridiculous and oppressive, and their advocates wicked or stupid or both. The sexual revolution is truly a revolution in that it has turned the moral world upside down.[17]

Trueman explains that the attitudes driving the sexual revolution stem from the changes in thinking regarding our sense of self—it is no longer connected to our biology, it is the prioritisation of the individual's inner psychology or what is described as 'feelings' or 'intuitions'. It is these internal 'feelings' that provide us with a sense of who we are and the purpose of our lives. In Trueman's words,

> Transgenderism provides an excellent example: people who think they are a woman trapped in a man's body are really making their inner psychological convictions absolutely decisive for who they are; and to the extent that, prior to coming out, they have publicly denied this inner reality; they have had an inauthentic existence. This is why the language of "living a lie" often appears in the testimonies of transgender people.[18]

To illustrate Trueman's analysis, I quote an insightful interview on YouTube with a young transgender man (that is, a biological female who transitioned to a man) who identifies as Christian. When giving the reason he transitioned, he stated,

> Because I wanted to show up more fully and completely as my internal sense of self. And the way we are in this Western society is that we place value judgements on what masculinity looks like and what femininity looks like, and I felt called to show more of this internal sense of masculinity. And I feel called to do something as simple as have less flesh on my chest or to simply, on a weekly basis, just take one injection of this much testosterone, and it happens to just grow facial hair; and that's the way that I best communicate to everyone else that my internal sense of self is masculine. I resonate in my spirit with that. ... I'm intending to present in the way that feels most in alignment with my internal

essence, and it just happens to—without any value judgement of negative or positive, or fear or judgement, or anything like that—resonate more with masculinity.[19]

Nancy Pearcey, in her book *Love Thy Body*, explains it from another angle. In today's culture there is a new orthodoxy or generally accepted theory—that the biological and psychological makeup of a person are not connected. She calls this the Personhood Theory and describes it as a body-person dichotomy, where the person has the moral and legal standing and the body is just an expendable biological organism.[20] Or in other words, it is like they are two different entities. That's why the person of a man can be born into a woman's body and the person of a woman can be born into a man's body.

This two-story division world view, with the person on a higher tier than the body, means that the mind—including its desires and feelings—has superiority over the body. That is why it is not the physical body that determines gender; it is the person or the mind.

Thus, we live in a day when parents have the huge responsibility to assign a 'gender' to their newborn babe at birth—legally and socially. At birth, they have to choose the likeliest gender identity, but 'if the children later tell us we are wrong, we shall then adjust accordingly'.[21]

A Secular Perspective

Apart from the gender confusion and fragmentation of today's young people, the sexual revolution has wrought a huge impact upon relationships between men and women. Author Heather Heying and evolutionary biologist Bret Weinstein, in an article titled, 'An Evolutionary Biologist's Guide to Finding Love in the 21st Century', provide an insightful perspective of the impact of birth control over the last fifty years. They believe that the invention of birth control destroyed the natural logic that directed sexual relationship norms.

> By freeing us to plan the timing and size of our families, reliable birth control has liberated women to strive and achieve alongside, and on par with, men. The gains in sexual equality that have been made in half a century are nothing short of staggering, largely due to birth control, and the benefit to humanity is all but undeniable.
>
> But that staggering benefit has come with staggering costs. As unfair as the pre-birth control world may have been, it had a recognizable logic to it. Sex was scarce because reproductive behavior carried sobering implications, especially for women who did not secure commitments from their partners in advance.[22]

Those sobering implications are conceiving and raising children. The authors explain that because of the unchangeable facts that men and women will be drawn to each other and that raising children is incredibly labour intensive, then women will be extremely careful about guarding themselves. In addition, a young woman was supported by her close kin, including her father—who had a more astute understanding of a man's instinct. (This sexual caution by women is what is meant by referring to women as sexual gatekeepers.) These sexual rules were written into every culture of civilisation and are reflected in the narratives and myths used to instruct societies. They continue in their article:

> Birth control — the ability to fully separate sex from reproduction — re-wrote those rules, suddenly, arbitrarily and irreversibly changing a fundamental part of human nature. That wasn't the intent, of course. It was supposed to give us power over our lives, and more of what is arguably the most rarefied and delightful

experience that people can have. And it did. But hyper-novel shifts carry enormous risks. And this shift wrecked the sexual logic that governed the system, providing nothing with which to replace it.[23]

The result of the dismantling of sacred institutions, the goal of the boomer elite, has decoupled sex from both reproduction and deep connectedness in relationship. This decoupling has fragmented men, women, and children. Children thrive best with a mother and father in a stable family, and even better in an extended family community. The authors state that the 'coherence of many systems is easily overlooked until it has been lost'. This is incredibly important. We have entered a new era that is incoherent and difficult to traverse. Heying and Weinstein write:

> And although the players [men and women] haven't gone anywhere, the rulebook was destroyed and replaced by an arbitrary and rapidly changing set of assertions made up by people who don't even seem to remember the objective of the exercise — to make and train our replacements so our lineage doesn't go extinct.[24]

As we considered at the beginning of this chapter, many millennials (but not the vast majority) are waking up to the chaos and the continual assault upon natural logic. They are tracing their heritage back to the firm bedrock of Judeo-Christian principles that formed the foundation of Western culture. The Western church has been ravaged by the sexualised culture, particularly our men and boys. This must be purposefully and urgently addressed in order for the church to be a faithful witness and display the glory of God in all purity.

1. Howard Markel, "The real story behind penicillin," PBS, September 27, 2013, https://www.pbs.org/newshour/health/the-real-story-behind-the-worlds-first-antibiotic.

2. Brian Alexander, "Free love: Was there a price to pay?" *NBC News*, June 22, 2007, http://www.nbcnews.com/id/19053382/ns/health-sexual_health/t/free-love-was-there-price-pay/#.WySE-1OFPVo.

3. Nalina Eggert, "Hugh Hefner death: Was the Playboy revolution good for women?" BBC, September 28, 2017, https://www.bbc.com/news/world-us-canada-41426299.

4. "How Playboy Became The World's Most Popular Magazine," FancyCrave, last updated March 8, 2022, https://fancycrave.com/playboy-magazine-history.

5. Jared Huff, "1960s – History Televised," The History of Television (October 21, 2017), https://historyoftelevisionblog.wordpress.com/2017/10/21/1960s-history-televised.

6. Temi Adebowale, "How the Hays Code—as Seen in *Hollywood*—Censored Hollywood," *Men's Health*, May 8, 2020, https://www.menshealth.com/entertainment/a32290089/hollywood-hays-code.

7. Britannica, T. Editors of Encyclopaedia, "MTV," *Britannica*, accessed May 7, 2022, https://www.britannica.com/topic/MTV.

8. Ben Shapiro, *Porn Generation: How Social Liberalism Is Corrupting Our Future* (Washington D.C.: Regnery Publishing, 2005), 2130.

9. Judith Adkins, "'These People Are Frightened to Death,'" *Prologue* magazine, National Archives, summer 2016, Vol. 48, No. 2. https://www.archives.gov/publications/prologue/2016/summer/lavender.html.

10. "The Gay Liberation Movement," University of Missouri-Kansas City, accessed October 20, 2021, https://info.umkc.edu/makinghistory/the-gay-liberation-movement.

11. Sue E. Browder, *Subverted: How I Helped the Sexual Revolution Hijack the Women's Movement* (San Francisco: Ignatius Press, 2019).

12. Mallory Millett, "Marxism Feminism's Ruined Lives," Mallory Millett.com, accessed May 7, 2022, https://mallorymillett.com/?p=37.

13. Ibid.

14. Tomas Chamorro-Premuzic, "The Tinder effect: psychology of dating in the technosexual era," *Guardian*, January 17, 2014, https://www.theguardian.com/media-network/media-network-blog/2014/jan/17/tinder-dating-psychology-technosexual.

15. *Merriam-Webster.com Dictionary*, s.v. "voyeurism," accessed February 11, 2022, https://www.merriam-webster.com/dictionary/voyeurism.

16. Cindy McGarvie, *Lost Boys: Bring Them Home* (New South Wales: Youth for Christ Australia, 2020), 27–28.

17. Trueman, 21–22.

18. Ibid., 23.

19. Anchored North, "Does God Love Trans People? Trans VS Ex-Trans," uploaded July 10, 2020, YouTube video, 13.20, https://www.youtube.com/watch?v=_nMMoWwDbbg.

20. Nancy R. Pearcey, *Love Thy Body: Answering Hard Questions about Life and Sexuality* (Grand Rapids: Baker Publishing Group, 2018), 18–19.

21. "Ethics of Gender Assignment," Intersex Society of North America, accessed February 3, 2022, https://isna.org/library/reinerprecepts.

22. Bret Weinstein and Heather Heying, "An Evolutionary Biologist's Guide to Finding Love in the 21st Century," *Daily Wire*, accessed April 27, 2022, https://www.dailywire.com/news/an-evolutionary-biologists-guide-to-finding-love-in-the-21st-century.

23. Ibid.

24. Ibid.

10

The Women's Liberation Movement

The women's movement is something that deeply interests me as I'm passionate about the flourishing of women. I recognise that women today are enjoying the opportunities, benefits, and protections won by women who have gone before us. I want to start this chapter by emphasising again that my aim is to look at the ideas driving today's feminist movement and lay out a challenge to examine them in light of its philosophy and the fruit—how women are faring today. It is my desire, too, that Christian women and the church might also discern ideas that they may have absorbed that undermine the high calling of women and motherhood.

As a broad overview, the women's movement has been recognised generally in three waves:

1. The right to vote and property rights in the late 1800s and early 1900s.

2. In the '60s and '70s—equality and anti-discrimination in education and the workforce.

3. From the 1990s—seeking to address things that some believed they missed in the first and the second waves. How so? Because the second wave was 'largely limited to White, college-educated women, and feminism failed to address the concerns of women of color, lesbians,

immigrants and religious minorities'.[1] In essence the various 'classes' of women are still oppressed.

During the second-wave struggle, female artists released powerful songs that became anthems for women of the day. From Lesley Gore's 1963 hit 'You Don't Own Me' to Nancy Sinatra's 1966 hit 'These Boots Are Made for Walkin'' to Helen Reddy's 1972 success 'I Am Woman', their lyrics were strong messages about female agency: the ability for a woman to make her own choices in life, her own goals, and her own decisions about her life and future. Women were seeking to break free and throw out the old traditional roles and expectations in relationships, social life, and the public sphere.

To be sure there was definitely much more reform to be won, but it seems that not all women were on the same page about what they actually wanted.

The 'Nameless Aching Dissatisfaction'

It was during the second wave of the women's movement when women began to challenge their traditional roles of wives, mothers, and homemakers. The angst behind this challenge came from the post-World War II '50s, when a woman's role was predominantly to get married, stay at home, raise her children, and not be the breadwinner. Some women struggled with this apparent 'simple and idyllic' lifestyle and began to ask questions. So when Betty Friedan published her book *The Feminine Mystique* in 1963, it identified a sense of emptiness in women that resonated strongly with some. Friedan called it 'this nameless aching dissatisfaction'.[2]

> The problem lay buried, unspoken for many years in the minds of American women. It was a strange stirring, a sense of dissatisfaction, a yearning that women suffered

> in the middle of the twentieth century in the United States.
>
> Each suburban wife struggled with it alone. As she made the beds, shopped for groceries, matched slipcover material, ate peanut butter sandwiches with her children, chauffeured Cub Scouts and Brownies, lay beside her husband at night—she was afraid to ask even of herself the silent question—'Is this all?'[3]

Friedan was able to define and articulate what she saw as the problem: 'the deeply engrained cultural belief that the only path to feminine fulfillment was to be a wife and mother'.[4] However, Friedan 'a fellow traveller of the Communist Party USA' was not forthright with the truth.

Helen Andrews writes that Freidan:

> claimed to have been alerted to the "problem that has no name" by a 1957 Smith alumnae questionnaire that showed her fellow members of the class of 1942 languishing in suburban misery, but she misrepresented the survey's findings. It actually showed that most respondents were satisfied with their marriages, felt perfectly free to work outside the home if they wanted to (most didn't), and generally had never been happier. Polls of suburban housewives in the 1960s found that compared with their working counterparts, they were more likely to report reading widely and to feel they were using their educations in their daily lives.[5]

To further her attack on women who chose to stay at home and care for their families, Friedan criticised the women's magazines of the day for promoting this cultural belief and thereby keeping women 'trapped in endless and empty housewifery'.[6]

She believed something needed to be done. And this is where the women's movement began to change course.

The Sexual Revolution and Women's Movement Unite

Sue Ellen Browder, a writer and trained investigative journalist who was right in the middle of the sexual revolution in New York City at the time, observed, 'In the beginning, the women's movement and the sexual revolution were *distinctly separate* cultural phenomena.'[7] The goal of the women's movement under the leadership of Betty Friedan was to attain equal opportunity for women in education and the workplace. Browder, a young writer for *Cosmo* at the time, observed that Betty Friedan called *Cosmo* 'quite obscene and quite horrible', referring to the blatant sexual promiscuity and glorifying of infidelity.[8] She also 'fought relentlessly against what she called "the bra-burning, anti-man politics of orgasm school" of feminism and warned younger women not to be seduced by the sex radicals' divisive rhetoric'.[9]

Browder explains:

> So how did the women's movement (which purportedly fought for women to be free to express their full personhood) and the sexual revolution (which reduced women to ambitious sex objects) become so intertwined in the popular mind that many young women today sincerely believe that to be "liberated" is to go to college, pursue a career, and be as sexually active as possible with no strings attached? How did these two separate revolutions get blended into one in a way that has led to so much pain for women and so much division within the churches and our society?[10]

The Next Revolution

She goes on to explain how Betty Friedan was convinced by her friend Larry Lader, a 'master propagandist skilled in the manipulation of public opinion', to graft abortion into the National Organisation for Women's political platform. Lader was an abortion activist and founder of the National Association for the Repeal of Abortion Laws, which evolved to what it is today—NARAL Pro-Choice America. Browder laments that the '1960s women's movement was hijacked largely due to the tireless efforts of one man, whose greatest passion was to make abortion legal'.[11]

Lader wrote a book titled *Abortion: The first authoritative and documented report on the laws and practices governing abortion in the U.S. and around the world, and how—for the sake of women everywhere—they can and must be reformed.*[12] In it he laid out how women, especially the poor, needed legalised abortion so that they could have complete feminine freedom. A phrase by Betty Friedan in her endorsement of the book emphasises that the abortion laws must be changed so that the state does not have the power to force women to 'bear a child against their will'. Lader developed the slogan 'No woman can call herself free who does not own and control her own body', which today has been shortened to 'My body, my choice'. And who can contend against that? As many who have studied propaganda know, slogans must be both vague (it doesn't mean anything or could mean everything) and inarguable, and this one was both. There are many slogans and narratives like this today, such as 'Love is love', used in the same-sex marriage campaigns that have been incredibly effective in diverting attention from the real questions and issues. But back to the story. How and when did the women's movement embrace abortion?

According to Browder, it happened at a meeting of the National Organisation of Women (NOW) on November 18th 1967, at their national conference. Betty Friedan introduced a resolution, the last one of the conference, to endorse abortion as a woman's legal right. What ensued was a 'bitter, strident controversy'. At the meeting, students and radicals showed up in unexpected numbers and at times became loud, and they stood and shouted, 'We've got to have an abortion plank!'[13] Many longstanding members of NOW were angry as they knew nothing about this resolution beforehand. At the end of the conference, the resolution was passed 57–14. With 105 women at the meeting, there is some controversy over there being only sixty-nine votes taken and the minutes recording taking ninety-seven votes. Nevertheless, fifty-seven women, many of them students and activists, changed the course of history. This meeting was believed to have been stacked and Friedan was accused of doing so.[14] Many women who had been strong members of NOW left the meeting in despair, many for good. 'For on that tragic night ... the women's movement was sharply scissored into two irreconcilable factions: women for legal abortion on demand, and women who opposed it.'[15]

At a media interview on the Monday after, Betty Freidan announced the new Bill of Rights, claiming to speak for '28 million working American women, the millions of women emerging from our colleges each year who are intent on full participation in the mainstream of our society, and mothers who are emerging from their homes to go back to school or work'.[16] So, from that time, on only fifty-seven votes at a controversial and railroaded meeting, the NOW claimed to be speaking for tens of *millions* of women. This opened the way for abortion law reform and other government and nongovernment organisations to repeal their laws. And the disappointing thing about this whole story is how a man behind the scenes was manipulating and influencing the women's movement.

Women's Liberation

Simultaneously, during these decades of second-wave feminism, the racial justice movement began calling themselves 'Black liberation'. This resonated particularly with the educated, elite women who wanted independence and freedom from what they describe as the 'oppression' of male supremacy.[17] Hence, the term 'women's liberation' was created parallel to the other liberation and freedom movements of the day.

The women's liberation movement (WLM) consisted of many feminist groups, such as NOW, and individuals who identified as standing for the rights of women. Each group had its own strategies for tackling injustices against women.

Germaine Greer was one of the radical leading voices of that era. She launched *The Female Eunuch* in 1970, which is still in print.[18] In it, she challenged traditional boundaries of female sexuality as patriarchal constructions and urged women to escape. Women already rebelled against traditional patriarchal views by getting medical assistance to suppress fertility and reproduction via the pill and abortion. More women were able to engage in casual sex outside marriage and have multiple partners without fear of pregnancy. Just like men.

Radical feminist writers and advocates of that era used Marxist ideas and tactics in their fight for the liberation of women from 'oppression'. They particularly developed the idea of 'false consciousness', which is about the masses not being aware that they are oppressed. Since they are unaware of their true state, they need to be 'awakened' to the social constructs that keep them oppressed. Observe the following definition from Britannica:

> False consciousness, in philosophy, particularly within critical theory and other Marxist schools and movements, the notion that members of the proletariat [working class] unwittingly misperceive their real

> position in society ... denotes people's inability to recognize inequality, oppression, and exploitation in a capitalist society because of the prevalence within it of views that naturalize and legitimize the existence of social classes.[19]

As an aside, it's important to note that according to Marxist ideology, 'oppression' is singularly identified to exist in capitalist societies. This raises the question that if capitalist societies are categorised as the most free, according to the World Freedom Index, and communist and socialist countries (developed upon Marxist ideology) measuring far less free, why does Marxist theory aim to dismantle capitalism?

But back to the point. The task of the second-wave feminists was to awaken the masses so they could rise up and break out of the oppressive patriarchal institutions that held them down, like marriage and homemaking, and move into male-dominated roles in the workforce and society instead. Carol Hanisch, a second-wave radical feminist, wrote an essay titled, 'The Personal is Political', which explained to women that all things in our private life are not private, but should be opened up to public scrutiny. Hanisch explains:

> Consciousness-raising was a way to use our own lives—our combined experiences—to understand concretely how we are oppressed and who was actually doing the oppressing. We regarded this knowledge as necessary for building such a movement.[20]

The phrases 'the personal is political' or 'private is political' became feminist slogans that voiced the idea that a woman's personal experiences are 'rooted in their political situation and gender inequality'.[21] Or that society consists of a system of power relationships, and where women sit in this system causes them to be oppressed, therefore it is a public and political issue.

And how would they do this consciousness-raising? Birthed in 1968 in New York City as a mass organising tool of the women's liberation movement, it expanded to the nation and the West in the form of 'consciousness-raising groups' for women. In an article explaining this, Carol Hanisch writes:

> In the autumn of 1968, [Kathie] Sarachild wrote up A Program for Feminist Consciousness-Raising to distribute at the first national women's liberation conference at Lake Villa near Chicago over Thanksgiving weekend. It initially received a mixed reception, but before long, even groups that had previously disparaged consciousness-raising as "therapy" or "navel-gazing" began to take it up. Consciousness-Raising swept the country, with groups in every major city and many smaller towns.[22]

Carol Hanisch is a founding member of New York Radical Women (1967). Her essay on consciousness-raising, 'The Personal Is Political', was published in 1969. The Carol Hanisch website brandishes a red-and-black banner with fists in the air, with the slogan 'Women of the World, Unite!'—a derivation of the Marxist 'Workers of the World, Unite!'[23]

Marxist ideology significantly informed the women's movement; there is no doubt about that. Joan Didion published her observation of the women's movement in the *New York Times* in 1972:

> "It is the right of the oppressed to organize around their oppression as they see and define it," the movement theorists insist doggedly in an effort to solve the question of these women, to convince themselves that what is going on is still a political process; but the handwriting is already on the wall. These are converts who want not a revolution but "romance," who believe

not in the oppression of women but in their own chances for a new life in exactly the mold of their old life. In certain ways they tell us sadder things about what the culture has done to them than the theorists ever did, and they also tell us, I suspect, that the women's movement is no longer a cause but a symptom.[24]

Has the women's movement that was hijacked by the elite, activist, academic women of the West contributed to the flourishing of women and children? Let history be the judge.

Reaping the Benefits Today

The efforts of the women's movement regarding equality in the workforce and education have been incredibly significant and have opened the paths for women to pursue pretty much any career they choose. Childcare, one of the key advocacy issues for the women's movement, has enabled more women to work and pursue careers outside the home. Government reforms for childcare assistance and maternity and paternity leave, and many other supports, also enable women to work outside the home.

Significant reforms were won by those in the women's movement who strongly opposed the abortion bill. For example, Elizabeth Boyer resigned from NOW's board of directors after that infamous meeting and founded the Women's Equity Action League (WEAL). Much of the membership of WEAL came from those disillusioned with the direction NOW had taken with reproductive 'rights' on abortion.[25] WEAL's strategy was to concentrate on education and the elimination of sex discrimination in the workforce. They were also instrumental in the passage of the Equal Credit Opportunity Act of 1974 that paved the way for married women to apply for credit in their own name.

Regarding the work equality issue, feminists and sympathisers today claim that there is a wage gap, meaning women are paid less then men, and this is a sign of continued discriminatory injustice against women. This message is carried through today's media to the public, providing 'consciousness-raising' for citizens on systemic inequality. However, the average person in the workforce knows that employers are bound under the law, particularly in Western nations, to pay correct wages.

A mathematical comparison was made between the average salary of a man and the average salary of a woman in full-time work, and it found that women earned $0.77 per every dollar a man earned. But this calculation does not indicate a wage injustice because the mathematical sum doesn't take into account occupation, education, or hours worked per week. Women tend to make different choices than men about hours they work, what jobs they tend to gravitate towards and so on. When they have children, women prefer to be at home more and choose jobs that allow for this. The wage gap myth was exposed by feminists back in 2014 when the American Association of University Women (AAUW) produced a study 'Graduating to a Pay Gap'.

> The AAUW has now joined ranks with serious economists who find that when you control for relevant differences between men and women (occupations, college majors, length of time in workplace) the wage gap narrows to the point of vanishing.[26]

It is perplexing as to why this divisive and emotive lie is still in circulation and used and repeated as a given truth. In addition, the inequality and suffering of women in other non-Western nations continues to persist without barely a peep from feminist activists. This blaring inconsistency exposes that the obsessive hostility towards capitalist societies from feminists is more about political ideology and power than helping women. It also exposes the maturation of Marxist ideological underpinnings of the feminist movement. On Australia's Green Left website, an article on women's liberation explains the wage gap in explicit Marxist terminology, particularly repeating words such as 'struggle' and 'ruling class'.

> However, while there may be widespread recognition of the concept of gender equality, women's lives are now getting harder, not easier. The gap between average male and female wages is increasing. Child care is unaffordable for many women ... Today's attacks on women are part and parcel of the broader neo-liberal offensive by the capitalist ruling class to further shift wealth from the poor to the rich through attacks on wages and conditions, privatisation of public utilities and cuts in government funding to social services.[27]

And these are the narratives that young women educated through our universities absorb and repeat. That article on Green Left's website was written in 1993 and is still on their website, at the time of writing, almost thirty years later! The emotive aspect of the narrative ensures that this lie is embedded deep in the consciousness of our girls and young women. It means that women see men as competitors, and this attitude is destructive for all relationships, from family to society. Women feel they are being 'attacked' as they try to live their day-to-day lives, so they have to be on guard to detect injustices towards them from an 'invisible' system.

Helen Andrews explains how the intent of pushing women into the workforce has had an impact on this generation of young mothers:

> The Baby Boomers are responsible for the difficulty that millennials have in making ends meet as a middle-class

couple, because they were the generation that sent women into the workforce en masse. Just as a statistical reality, very few families were dual earner families in 1960 and nowadays most of them are. And so that switch happened over the course of the Baby Boomer generation. Elizabeth Warren coined the term, the "two-income trap" for what happened when women flooded into the workforce in the seventies and eighties, which simply bid up the price of a middle-class living. So nobody was actually economically better off because all the women entered the workforce at the same time, and so the two-income trap means that the cost of a middle-class lifestyle now requires two incomes whereas it didn't before.[28]

Life has become exhausting, but there's more. What about the sexual revolution aspect of the women's liberation movement?

The Fallout of Feminism's Sexual Freedom Advocacy and Consciousness-Raising

Looking around, fifty years after the second-wave feminist sexual revolution, we see that:

- Domestic violence against women has increased.
- Objectification of women through pornography and marketing is a norm.
- Prostitution has been legalised whereby women can be paid to be used and abused by men.
- Abortions are legal and subsidised by the government.
- Sexual abuse cases have exploded.

The Women's Liberation Movement

- A significant number of perpetrators are kids sexually abusing other kids on playgrounds at school.
- Our girls are exposed to vulgar and perverse sexual inuendo daily at school.
- Girls are becoming sexually active at a younger age as well as dressing provocatively beyond their years.
- Young girls are viewing porn at record rates.
- Sex education in schools encourages sexual activity and equips girls with how to do it without getting pregnant, but if they do, they are instructed where to go to have a 'termination'.

The list continues.

Our world has become super sexualised, and women and children suffer the most. But the blame does not solely sit at the feet of men. Women have played a major role too.

So many books have been written on the devastation caused by feminist ideology and how it has shipwrecked so many women's lives. Women have found themselves still working beyond childbearing age, unmarried, desperately lonely, or divorced. Many marriages have become a combat zone to ensure each partner is contributing their equal 50 per cent of the housework, finances, and childcare. As mentioned earlier, economically, many mothers no longer have the choice to stay at home and raise their children. This is a great loss for families.

> Women have always worked, but never in American history did women outnumber men in the labor force until January 2020. Boomers promised that employment was the only way for women to be fulfilled and independent, when any socialist could have told them that there is no one more dependent than a wage worker.[29]

Women were sold a lie by the elites of the feminist movement—the lie that a woman's true value and identity is in her career and work outside the home with the *workers of the world*. Parents of today and, yes, the church too, have failed to counteract the pervasive lies and misrepresentations that all women need to be in the workplace.

> This cultural dogma is so pervasive and so uncontested that it induces young women, not quite onboard with the program, to cauterize their hearts and pursue a life unnatural to them, often leaving them frustrated, anxious and bitter.[30]

Marriage coach and author Suzanne Venker, in her book *How to Get Hitched and Stay Hitched: A 12-Step Program for Marriage-Minded Women* (2021), identifies four lies of the culture that have their origins in the feminist ideology that she constantly sees in her counselling sessions, or in the hundreds of email letters she receives. These four lies perpetrated by feminists are:

1. Marriage + motherhood = jail,
2. Women should never depend on a man.
3. Sex is just sex.
4. Career success will and should define them.[31]

Venker states on her podcast:

> The women who fell for these lies are now picking up the pieces of a life gone awry, a life that is not working, usually for one of two reasons: They either can't find a marriageable man or do find one but are unable to have children the natural way, or to stay home with the children they do have despite their desire to do so. That is precisely because they prioritized career over marriage and were groomed to ignore, as Heindricks points out

> "the constraints of time and biology." And for what? For what? For a political agenda. Feminists may want all the women in the world in the workplace so they can feel less alone and so they can push through their agenda for childcare and paid leave and all the rest. But that is not what most women want, nor is it good for children and families. Unfortunately, it is very difficult to go against the grain when it appears that everyone else around you is doing something contrary to what you want, that's why it's so critical we turn this mess around.[32]

Venker goes on to explain that in 2020, the birth rate in the US was the lowest ever in more than a century, and this was not due to the pandemic. It was due to the fact that women are waiting longer to marry and having far fewer children than their mothers and grandmothers. The reason for this, says Venker, is that they have been 'groomed to put marriage and motherhood on the backburner to pursue money and career instead. But not only are the values out of sync with nature, they've also come with enormous psychological cost for men, children, families, society, and even women'.[33]

It surely is time to turn this mess around. The feminist movement does not produce happy women. In fact, Betty Friedan's lament is repeating itself again—the modern woman today lies in bed alone at night and is 'afraid to ask even of herself the silent question—Is this all?'.

A Biblical Perspective

Discipleship of our children is first and foremost the role of Christian parents. From birth to young adult, parents have the chief responsibility to train their children. It's hard work and takes concentrated effort. Mothers play a significant role in those early infant years and throughout childhood, as expressed so beautifully in the poem by William Ross Wallace (1819–1891) 'The Hand That Rocks the Cradle Rules the World'. The second to last stanza reads:

> *Woman, how divine your mission,*
> *Here upon our natal sod;*
> *Keep—oh, keep the young heart open*
> *Always to the breath of God!*
> *All true trophies of the ages*
> *Are from mother-love impearled,*
> *For the hand that rocks the cradle*
> *Is the hand that rules the world.*[34]

The feminist philosophy is in opposition to motherhood. It teaches that a woman's place is outside the home in the workforce, and that is where she finds her worth. So sadly, the hand that rocks the cradle is the young girl at the day care centre. The lie of feminism that deceives today's generations is diametrically opposed to the mission of biblical motherhood. To cast a glimpse at what biblical motherhood and homemaking looks like, Proverbs 31 is a beautiful and honouring picture of a wife of noble character.

She is a rarity and her worth is 'far above rubies', her husband has full confidence in her, 'her children arise and call her blessed', she oversees her household with diligence, she works hard and is gifted, she is dressed beautifully in fine linen, she buys fields and grows her own, she runs her own business from home, she opens her arms to the poor and needy, she fears God, she faithfully instructs her family, she has strength and dignity and can laugh at the days to come, and much more.

This is an incredibly empowering picture of motherhood (and womanhood) that encompasses women flourishing spiritually, emotionally, physically, socially, and materially. I have never seen such high regard for the woman written or spoken of before in history, not even amongst the most highly acclaimed feminist advocates of all time.

The church must encourage, honour, and support the role of motherhood and do whatever it can to help mothers who want to stay at home. Older women must teach the younger women how to respect their husbands and train their children. This in turn will strengthen the Christian family and home life, thereby strengthening the church and the community.

Women, resist the lies of the world. Rise up and take your noble place, embrace your divine mission as it is honourable and virtuous. Your children will surely one day arise and call you blessed!

---

1. Editors, "Feminism," History.com, last updated April 8, 2022, https://www.history.com/topics/womens-history/feminism-womens-history.
2. Ibid.
3. Betty Friedan, *The Feminine Mystique*, 2nd ed. (Scranton, Pennsylvania: W. W. Norton & Company, 1963), 15.
4. Browder, 17.
5. Andrews, 5.
6. Browder, 17.
7. Browder, 11.
8. Ibid., 12.
9. Ibid.
10. Ibid.
11. Ibid., 15.
12. Lawrence Lader, *Abortion* (Indianapolis, Indiana: Bobbs-Merrill, 1966).
13. Browder, 66.
14. Ibid., 70.
15. Ibid.
16. Ibid., 71.
17. Linda Napikoski, "Women's Liberation Movement — Definition and Overview," ThoughtCo., last updated September 10, 2019, https://www.thoughtco.com/womens-liberation-movement-3528926.
18. Germaine Greer, "Germaine Greer & The Female Eunuch," *Ergo*, accessed April 7, 2018, http://ergo.slv.vic.gov.au/explore-history/fight-rights/womens-rights/germaine-greer-female-eunuch.

19. Britannica, T. Editors of Encyclopaedia, "false consciousness," *Britannica*, accessed May 6, 2022, https://www.britannica.com/topic/false-consciousness.

20. Holly Hammond, "Consciousness Raising," The Commons Social Change Library, accessed August 2, 2021, https://commonslibrary.org/consciousness-raising.

21. Christopher J. Kelly, "the personal is political," *Britannica*, accessed May 6, 2022, https://www.britannica.com/topic/the-personal-is-political.

22. Carol Hanisch, "Women's Liberation Consciousness-Raising: Then and Now," *On The Issues* magazine, accessed August 2, 2021, https://www.ontheissuesmagazine.com/2010spring/2010spring_Hanisch.php.

23. See www.carolhanisch.org.

24. Joan Didion, "The Women's Movement," *New York Times*, July 30, 1972, https://www.nytimes.com/1972/07/30/archives/the-womens-movement-women.html.

25. Candis Steenbergen, "Women's Equity Action League," *Britannica*, accessed May 7, 2022, https://www.britannica.com/topic/Womens-Equity-Action-League.

26. Christina Hoff Sommers, "Wage Gap Myth Exposed — By Feminists," *HuffPost*, November 4, 2012, https://www.huffpost.com/entry/wage-gap_b_2073804.

27. Kerryn Williams, "Women's liberation," Green Left, Issue 574 (November 17, 1993), https://www.greenleft.org.au/content/womens-liberation.

28. Stuckey, "Blaming Boomers."

29. Andrews, chapter 1.

30. Rebeccah L. Heinrichs, "Baby Bust," Hudson Institute, accessed May 7, 2022, https://www.hudson.org/research/16937-baby-bust.

31. Suzanne Venker, "The Suzanne Venker Show: 111. 4 Lies the Culture Tells Women," Apple Podcasts podcast, 12:00, accessed August 31, 2021, https://podcasts.apple.com/vn/podcast/111-4-lies-the-culture-tells-women/id1471433977?i=1000533860679.

32. Ibid.

33. Ibid.

34. "The Hand that Rocks the Cradle by William Wallace (1819–1881)," Women of Christianity, June 2, 2018, https://womenofchristianity.com/the-hand-that-rocks-the-cradle-by-william-ross-wallace-1819-1881.

— 11 —

The Environmental Movement

The environment is on the forefront of every domain, from government and education to the everyday person at the grocery store. It's a huge issue that has been very divisive, particularly in the last decade. Young people today carry a huge burden. The fear, uncertainty, and doubt that come with apocalyptic warnings are heavy loads to bear. The added pandemic alarmism is not unlike other apocalyptic messages affecting our young people in that it has also cultivated an underlying mood of hopelessness.

I've already discussed how environmentalism has become a religion to some. However, this chapter examines the birth of the modern environmental movement which took off during the '60s and '70s. Again, it is necessary to state that I recognise the need for an environmental and conservationist movement and applaud the fact that the West is now very conscious of stewarding our environment well. This chapter is a brief dive into the philosophy driving the movement today.

Scripture has much to say about the environment or creation, as it is called, and I discuss a Christian response at the end of the chapter.

The '70s Ice Age Scare

When I began researching for this chapter, I was motivated by a stark memory in my childhood (in the late '70s) of when our science teacher told us the distressing news that the world was about to enter another ice age. I was devastated to hear this, and it left me depressed and anxious, with some heavy questions about life that I carried alone and didn't discuss with anyone who might have been able to help me. Why did I have to be born into this apocalyptic age?

And there was not one thing we could do to stop it happening.

I carried this underlying heaviness around for many years until one day I realised that I hadn't heard anyone mention the impending ice age for a long time. Relieved, I assumed that we had somehow escaped it and that I needn't worry any longer, so I looked to the future with hope.

Turns out that in 1971, some scientists from NASA wrote papers on a *possible* coming ice age because global temperatures had been falling since 1940. The media got a hold of it and sensationalised the coverage.[1] Apparently, these scientists got their figures wrong but didn't send the memo to the rest of the world, or perhaps it just wasn't deemed media worthy. Whatever the case, many of us early Gen Xers and late boomers remember the ice age scare.

Then came a new apocalyptic warning: the earth isn't cooling, it's warming, and humankind is the cause. And we've heard more recent declarations that we only have twelve years left.[2] Snow caps are melting, polar bears are dying, plastic straws are killing our sea life, our carbon footprint is too high, and on and on.

There is so much to be concerned about, and young people need some hope because they deeply care about the earth and their future world.

From Conservationism to Environmentalism

In the '60s, environmentalism took off with the real scare of a nuclear holocaust and a strong push against war. Until then, people who cared about the environment and wanted to protect nature were called conservationists or naturalists. Environmentalism, as with all *isms* is about a belief system, and it became much more rigid in its beliefs—making it much more like a religion, as previously discussed.

Dr. Patrick Moore, one of the co-founders of Greenpeace, recounts how the activist group was birthed. Moore, with a posse of others, hired a boat to go to an American nuclear test site in Alaska to protest there and hopefully stop the testing of the H-bomb. They were concerned not just about the ecological affects but also the human devastation of nuclear bombs used in war. They were all aware of what happened at Hiroshima, and with the Cuban missile crisis threat so fresh in their memories, they became pacifists and wanted to do something. Although their efforts were not successful in stopping the testing, they received good media attention back in the US, which raised awareness significantly. Soon after, President Nixon cancelled further tests. Moore recounts how they were encouraged by the overwhelming support to stop the H-bomb testing and its subsequent outcome. It was from this experience that Greenpeace was formed in 1971.

Moore records in his book *Confessions of a Greenpeace Dropout: The making of a sensible environmentalist* his view on the times:

> The last half of the 20th century was marked by a revulsion for war and a new awareness of the environment. Beatniks, hippies, eco-freaks, and greens in their turn fashioned a new philosophy that embraced

> peace and ecology as the overarching principles of a civilized world. Spurred by more than 30 years of ever-present fear that global nuclear holocaust would wipe out humanity and much of the living world, we led a new war—a war to save the earth. I've had the good fortune to be a general in that war ... We campaigned against the bomb makers, whale-killers, polluters, and anyone else who threatened civilization or the environment. In the process we won the hearts and minds of people around the world. We were Greenpeace.[3]

As you would have noticed by the title of Moore's book, he is no longer with Greenpeace today. After fifteen years, they separated ways with Moore, stating that Greenpeace left him as they became increasingly senseless by adopting an 'agenda that is antiscience, antibusiness, and downright antihuman'.[4] However, the good work that was done in raising awareness on the global level—forcing industries to clean up their acts and stop forming toxic waste dumps—has been important. In 1975, Greenpeace stood against huge factory whaling fleets, and in the 1980s, they confronted the annual slaughter of baby seals. They successfully used the power of worldwide media to get attention from governments of industrialised democracies.

By 1982, Greenpeace International was bringing in $100 million a year in donations, but at that time, Moore struggled with two issues:

- The first was the opposition to the concept of sustainable development. Greenpeace was anti-development, so those in developing nations were hindered from moving forward in implementing better practices and technologies, thus preventing them from lifting people out of poverty. Moore sympathised with the issues facing poorer nations.

In addition, he saw sustainable development to be more of a challenge to tackle because it entailed 'consensus and cooperation rather than confrontation and demonization'.⁵ Moore believed that Greenpeace's goal of getting Western nations to consider the importance of the environment had mostly been achieved and felt it was no longer necessary to keep 'beating them over the head with it'. He wanted them to now sit down and discuss and look for solutions together.

- The second issue Moore struggled with was the adoption of policies that he felt were extremist and irrational. He experienced his boomer colleagues becoming 'more extreme and intolerant of dissenting opinions within'. Since Western democracies adopted many of the Greenpeace environment agendas, their demands became even more over the top, and Moore believes that those in Greenpeace 'couldn't make the transition from confrontation to consensus'.

The eighties ended with the fall of communism and the end of the Cold War, and the peace movement with its rather anti-American leanings was pretty much disbanded. Many of its members moved to the environmental movement, 'bringing with them their neo-Marxist, far-left agendas'. Moore believes that the environmental movement was 'hijacked by political and social activists who learned to use green language to cloak agendas that had more to do with anticapitalism and anti-globalization than with science and ecology'.⁶

Moore recalls visiting the Greenpeace Toronto office in 1985 and meeting new recruits, many of whom were dressed in 'army fatigues and red berets in support of the Sandinistas' (a Nicaraguan Marxist resistance group by the name of National Liberation Front).

He laments in his 2021 book *Fake Invisible Catastrophes and Threats of Doom*, 'Unfortunately, Greenpeace had gone from an altruistic group of volunteers with a noble vision, to a business with an ever-expanding budget, a matching payroll to meet, and it was now rapidly transforming into a racket peddling junk science.'[7]

Real Threats or Not?

The late novelist and filmmaker Michael Crichton (with an MD from Harvard Medical School and also graduating in anthropology) gave a renowned speech in 2003 that people are still quoting today. I encourage you to read it as it was incredibly enlightening, even prophetic for someone who was not a Christian and quite against religion in all respects. He first claims that 'the greatest challenge facing mankind is the challenge of distinguishing reality from fantasy, truth from propaganda … We must daily decide whether the threats we face are real, whether the solutions we are offered will do any good, whether the problems we're told exist are in fact real problems, or non-problems'.[8] He is, of course, referring to many of the campaigns of environmentalists since this movement began. Like Patrick Moore, he was also deeply concerned about the direction the environmental movement was heading. He felt that it was too politicised and had become a religion.

Crichton mentions a number of the nonfactual environmental campaigns that led to what he believes caused the deaths of 10 to 30 million people since the 1970s. One of the major ones he highlights, and one that many of us remember, is the DDT campaign. DDT is a synthetic insecticide which had been used with great effect to combat mosquito-borne diseases. In 1972, DDT was successfully banned as a carcinogen. Crichton purports that those who banned it knew specifically that it was not carcinogenic but were not swayed by facts.

The DDT campaign began in 1962 with a book published by the late Rachel Carson titled *Silent Spring*—about the damage of man-made pesticides on the environment, particularly wildlife. It was her arguments that were instrumental in the banning of DDT in the US and, subsequently, for the World Health Organization to ban it internationally as well.

As a result, Crichten says this ban:

> has caused the deaths of tens of millions of poor people, mostly children, whose deaths are directly attributable to a callous, technologically advanced western society that promoted the new cause of environmentalism by pushing a fantasy about a pesticide, and thus irrevocably harmed the third world. Banning DDT is one of the most disgraceful episodes in the twentieth century history of America. We knew better, and we did it anyway, and we let people around the world die and didn't give a damn.[9]

I saw this firsthand in Africa, where people are still dying by the score, particularly the vulnerable, the sick, and the children from the insect-borne disease of malaria. Millions in poverty do not have access to medical treatment or the mosquito nets that were the alternative solution to DDT. Malaria could have been controlled decades ago with DDT.

> DDT was extremely successful in controlling malaria in the middle of the 20th century, and WHO actively promoted its use for this until the early 1980s. But increased health and environmental concerns surrounding DDT caused WHO to stop promoting it and to focus instead on the other two main

interventions to fight malaria (drug treatment and insecticide treated bed nets).

Deaths from malaria have continued to rise since the 1970s, however, and countries affected by the disease and members of the scientific community have demanded that DDT should be used again for inside residual spraying. Additionally, extensive research and testing ... have shown that well managed programmes of spraying DDT indoors pose no harm to humans or to wildlife.[10]

On examining some of the charts on malaria mortality in the 20th century, one cannot help but notice its stark rise since 1970. One must agree with Crichton that this has indeed been a tragedy, and the poorest of the poor have suffered the most.

Earth Day: Bringing the Environment to the Fore

The first Earth Day was celebrated on 22 April 1970, with millions of Americans, many of them young people from universities, marching for the environment. It was the idea of Senator Gaylord Nelson, who said, "'The objective was to get a nationwide demonstration of concern for the environment so large that it would shake the political establishment out of its lethargy," Senator Nelson said, "and, finally, force this issue permanently onto the national political agenda.'"[11]

Today environmentalism has proliferated. It is now embedded 'permanently onto the national political agenda'. Also now, environmentalism is on the worldwide government agenda. The amount of environmental advocacy groups is staggering. There are thousands, from Friends of the Earth to the latest radical

The Environmental Movement

group Extinction Rebellion, which one British columnist described as an 'upper-middle-class death cult'.[12]

The USA reported that in the ten-year period from 2005 to 2015, the largest proportional increase in revenue was first religion-related charities. That's all religious charities, such as Salvos, food banks, pregnancy support centres, homelessness charities, poverty relief initiatives, medical support initiatives, and so on. Very close behind were environmental and animal organisations.[13] The environmental movement is a huge money-making industry.

These organisations attract young people, and from what I observed when visiting their websites, are aimed specifically towards this demographic.

The concern over the environment is absolutely necessary, but something has gone drastically wrong. Over thirty-three years later, Crichton laments (along with many others) that environmentalism has turned into a religion:

> Today, one of the most powerful religions in the Western World is environmentalism. Environmentalism seems to be the religion of choice for urban atheists. Why do I say it's a religion? Well, just look at the beliefs. If you look carefully, you see that environmentalism is in fact a perfect 21st century remapping of traditional Judeo-Christian beliefs and myths.[14]

Crichton goes on to explain the similarities. I encourage you to read his perspective.

The Christian Response

There seems to be an obvious subliminal conflict between the Christian faith and the environmental movement. Christian young people have no idea how to reconcile the narrative they hear in mainline culture with their Christian beliefs. They care deeply about the environment and are backed into a corner, where they either accept the world's messages and outlook or they are an enemy of the earth. Again, this comes down to teaching and instructing, particularly addressing the issues that are dominating discourse, directing development, and guiding decisions for the future. Besides the obvious differences in the spiritual aspects of environmentalism, it is not clear to Christians, particularly in this age, how we relate to the environment (or creation) physically. This issue should be of paramount importance for churches. Our young people need answers urgently. Since they haven't been given anything adequate, their Christian faith becomes irrelevant and they look to the world for answers.

So does the Bible have answers? And if so, is there evidence of both humanity and creation flourishing together?

There are so many valuable resources on this topic, such as the Disciple Nations Alliance—leading Christian thinkers on development who I highly recommend. They provide resources that record incredible stories of societal transformation through adopting biblical environment-stewarding practices. Disciple Nations Alliance leaders have explained this issue so well and with such hope that I use their explanations in this section.

Before I do so, it is important to note there are Christians (and those who don't hold Judeo-Christian beliefs) doing incredible work in agriculture, industry, development, and science who would call themselves conservationists and environmentalists without embracing the religious aspects of environmentalism. It's just that they are not the ones who have the platform.

Darrow Miller of Disciple Nations Alliance explains that many Christians operate from the 'Evangelical Gnostic paradigm that separates the spiritual from the physical'.[15] This plays out by only bringing a 'spiritual' solution and the narrow gospel of salvation to real-life problems like development and agriculture. People need to live, plant and harvest, and take care of their families. Real-life, practical problems need real-life solutions, and a narrow gospel solution is inadequate. On the other hand, the secular solution to poverty, modern development, and agriculture has been a physical one. This encompasses funds, machinery, technical help, and resources—all good but with no transformation of life and communities and no flourishing of humanity. This is evidenced by the billions of dollars of aid sent to developing nations over decades and little development happening. Some even call places like Africa a black hole, where funds disappear.

There is also the environmentalist approach that purports that since man is like a 'cancer' on the earth, he should only take what he needs, avoid development, and live as one with nature. This approach believes that in the end, man must diminish in order to save Mother Earth.[16]

Miller explains in his article 'Agriculture and the Kingdom of God' that Christians have a faulty world view that has 'left much of the church functioning from a Gnostic paradigm in its religious life and the cultural paradigm (secularism or animism) in the rest of her life'. Simply, the church has absorbed another philosophy, and that is the separation of the spiritual and physical—the physical being of lesser importance. Therefore less respect is given to the physical instead of understanding that creation was given to man to steward and care for, and this is a reflection of our worship of God.[17]

The biblical view, according to Miller, is that man relates upwardly to God as his creator, and because God owns creation, man relates to creation as its steward. He unpacks it this way:

There are two aspects of this stewardship, societal and developmental.

The Societal Mandate is established by the biblical statement, "be fruitful, increase in number, and fill the earth." To develop the earth there must be families, communities and societies. Adam and Eve were to have children and populate the earth. But fill the earth with what? It depends on your worldview. The filling of the earth is not with "consumers" as the materialist would say. Nor is it with "human spirits" that have no interest in the physical world. The mandate is to fill the earth with image bearers of God; it is to fill the earth with agriculturists and horticulturists, artists and painters, composers and poets, architects and craftsman. Fill the earth with families and communities of stewards.

The Development Mandate is established by the words rule and subdue, and later, in Genesis 2:15, with work and care. These words "rule" and "subdue" reflect that man is to have dominion over creation rather than the other way around as the animists and their New Age counterparts in the ecological movement would argue. The word "work" reflects that man is to progress, to expand and advance the garden, not to leave it as he found it. The word "care" reflects that man is to conserve—to protect and cherish the garden—to keep it healthy and thriving. This is in contrast with our consumer oriented materialistic culture that simply wants to harvest, deplete, use, and too often, rape creation.

The development mandate to progress and conserve is beautifully balanced. It stands in stark contrast to secularism's focus on "working but not caring" which can result in the abuse of creation. On the other hand it also contrasts New Age ecology movement which focuses on caring for, but not working the garden. This leads to underdevelopment. The development mandate celebrates imago Dei, calling man to expand the garden, create orchards, discover the wonders of creation through science, and to fill the earth with the knowledge of God! Worship leads to development.[18]

And this offers so much hope!

> *'All the earth worships you and sings praises to you; they sing praises to your name'* (Psalm 99:4 ESV).

---

1. Michael Le Page, "Climate myths: They predicted global cooling in the 1970s," *New Scientist*, May 16, 2007, https://www.newscientist.com/article/dn11643-climate-myths-they-predicted-global-cooling-in-the-1970s.
2. John Bowden, "Ocasio-Cortez: 'World will end in 12 years' if climate change not addressed," *The Hill*, January 22, 2019, https://thehill.com/policy/energy-environment/426353-ocasio-cortez-the-world-will-end-in-12-years-if-we-dont-address.
3. Patrick A. Moore, *Confessions of a Greenpeace Dropout: The Making of a Sensible Environmentalist* (British Colombia, Canada: Beatty Street Publishing, 2010).
4. Ibid.
5. Ibid., 12.
6. Ibid., 14.
7. Patrick A. Moore, *Fake Invisible Catastrophes and Threats of Doom* (Capetown, South Africa: EcoSense Environmental Incorporated, 2021), 10.
8. Michael Crichton, "Remarks to the Commonwealth Club," Carnegie Mellon University, September 15, 2003, https://www.cs.cmu.edu/~kw/crichton.html.
9. Crichton, "Remarks."
10. Christiane Rehwagen, "WHO recommends DDT to control malaria," National Library of Medicine, BMJ (Sep 23, 2006); 333(7569): 622, https://www.ncbi.nlm.nih.gov/pmc/articles/PMC1570869.

11. "The first Earth Day," This Day in History, History.com, accessed May 7, 2022) https://www.history.com/this-day-in-history/the-first-earth-day.

12. Shellenberger, 270.

13. Brice S. McKeever, "The Nonprofit Sector in Brief 2018," National Center for Charitable Statistics, December 13, 2018, https://nccs.urban.org/publication/nonprofit-sector-brief-2018#the-nonprofit-sector-in-brief-2018-public-charites-giving-and-volunteering.

14. Crichton, "Remarks."

15. Darrow L. Miller, "Agriculture and the Kingdom of God," Disciple Nations Alliance, last updated April 2020, https://disciplenations.org/wp-content/uploads/2020/04/Agriculture-and-the-Kingdom-of-God.pdf.

16. Ibid., 3.

17. Ibid., 6.

18. Ibid., 6–7.

— 12 —

The Antiwar Movement

This chapter is important because it provides a glimpse into the unrest and tension (on the world stage and at home) during the Vietnam War. Young people, the baby boomers, were impacted considerably, particularly since their young men were drafted into a war that didn't seem to have anything to do with them. This impacted the young boomers at the time, and together with the ideas that they embraced, it shaped their negative attitude towards America and the West—which was not there with previous generations. And they passed this on to the next generations. In addition, the fear and tension of war and unrest—the existential crisis— contributed to the social environment in which the Jesus revolution broke out, so we must pay attention since we live in a similar era.

I begin with John Lennon, the man who thought religion should die.

John Lennon's song 'Imagine', released in 1971 during the heaviest fighting period in Vietnam, was considered the 'atheist's anthem'. He stated that his song was 'anti-religious, anti-nationalistic, anti-conventional, anti-capitalistic ... but because it is sugar-coated, it is accepted'.[1]

The Vietnam War issue was complex and deeply connected to the social unrest of the times. It was the war that the hippies fought at home against the government through antiwar demonstrations and protests.

> The war cannot be isolated from the pervasive turmoil that rolled through the American home front in the 1960s: the antiwar movement, escalating racial tensions, the rise of the hippie counterculture, the wave of conservative backlash, and the growing cynicism about the government and cultural authorities of every kind.[2]

Vietnam was just one of the many proxy wars of the Cold War, which lasted from just after the end of World War II (1948) through to the collapse of the Soviet Union in 1991. The Cold War was fought between the US and her allies and the Soviet Union and her allies. If you've never studied it, then I encourage you to do so as it will help you make more sense of the world today.[3]

This Cold War wasn't fought directly, in the physical sense, between the US and USSR, but the war involved several tactics. These included an arms race—a competitive effort to build the most powerful weapons of destruction—and the fighting of proxy wars around the world in countries that supported either communism or capitalism. Vietnam was just one of those wars. Young people in the 1960s were very much seeking and desiring world peace, particularly after the scare of the Cuban Missile Crisis in 1962, when it was discovered that the Soviets had planted intercontinental ballistic missiles in Cuba and were within reach of launching an attack on US cities.

The assassination of President John F. Kennedy on 22 November 1963 was one of those moments in life when people remember exactly where they were when they heard the news. Kennedy's accused killer, Lee Harvey Oswald, was said to have embraced Marxism and defected for a time to the Soviet Union. Oswald was shot and killed when in custody, so he never stood trial, and the truth went with him to the grave.

This invisible war lasted for forty-five years and was an ever-present, background tension for those who lived through those times. It finally ended with an unexpected crash when the Berlin Wall fell in 1989, followed by the collapse of the Soviet Union in 1991. With that background, let's take a closer look at the antiwar movement, particularly the counter-culture hippies. Who were they and what was their motivation?

Antiwar, Flower Power Hippies

Hippies were the generation following the beatniks, who have an anti-establishment history of their own. Hippies were of the baby boomer generation. They rejected the establishment and its norms and were much more active than the beatniks in expressing their public dissent against the institutions of the day. Like today's politically driven young people within university environments, the hippie movement had much of its origins on college campuses in the US. Many hippies were ultimately college dropouts. They had managed to encounter a lot of new intellectual input that not only questioned traditional values and Western civilisation but also generated hostility towards their own nation.

Camille Paglia provides a good insight about the hippies and their political activism, which was mixed with spiritualism:

> Members of the sixties counterculture were passionately committed to political reform, yet they were also seeking the truth about life outside religious and social institutions. Despite their ambivalence toward authority, however, they often sought gurus—mentors or guides, who sometimes proved fallible. One problem was that the more the mind was opened to what was commonly called "cosmic consciousness" (a hippie rubric of the sixties), the less meaningful politics or

> social structure became, melting into the Void. Civil rights and political reform are in fact Western ideals: Hinduism and Buddhism, by extinguishing the ego and urging acceptance of ultimate reality, see suffering and injustice as essential conditions of life that cannot be changed but only endured.[4]

The hippie movement was very eclectic in its makeup and experience. Hippie enclaves were a mish-mash of university dropouts, society's disillusioned, and runaways; mixed with the culture of the day, drugs, music, and current events.

Many people remember hippies as young people with tie-dyed clothes, beads, no shoes, and long, often unkempt hair. They usually took drugs and lived communally. Many came from middle-class and wealthy families that had placed a lot of pressure on them to succeed. Their aim was to live carefree and simple lives, unlike their middle- to upper-class parents, who seemed to have wealth but were still unhappy and not doing what they really wanted in life.[5] They critically referred to people who weren't hippies as 'squares'; conformist, conservative, predictable, and not very interesting.

In their antiwar activism, hippies were sometimes referred to as 'flower children' because they used flowers as a symbol of peace—often wearing them in their hair and distributing them to the public.[6] They were often remembered as placing flowers in the barrels of rifles held by soldiers on military parades.

But what was this war they protested, and how did it shape the world at the time?

Vietnam, the Unpopular War

America's initial involvement in the Vietnam War (1955–1975) was in a military assistance and advisory capacity, and that's what the American people understood it to be.[7] But in 1965,

THE ANTIWAR MOVEMENT

the situation transformed into a full-scale war that snuck up on everyone. Between 1965 and 1973, the war was at its most violent. By 1966, Pentagon sources were reporting 254,000 US troops in Vietnam with another 90,000 'performing tasks directly concerned with the escalating war effort'.[8] President Lyndon B. Johnson was accused of 'deceiving Congress and the American people by hiding the true cost of the Vietnam War'.[9] By the time the war was over, 58,000 had lost their lives, over 300,000 were wounded, and 2.7 million Americans had served. Amputations and crippling wounds were 300% higher than during World War II.[10]

The war situation caused the American people much angst. It was a very divisive time. The college professors and leftist organisations on campuses, as well as prominent celebrities and Democrat politicians, protested together with the hippies against the war. The most memorable hippie slogan was 'Make love, not war'. The media was also a strong and relentless opponent of Republican President Nixon and the Vietnam War.

In addition, about one third of soldiers were drafted—men aged 18–25 years were called up for compulsory service. The draft boards consisted of local community members who had incredible power to decide a young man's draft status—whether they should go or could stay—and these boards could be pressured.

> Most of U.S. soldiers drafted during the Vietnam War were men from poor and working-class families. These were young men who were not going get a college deferment, have a political connection, or have a family doctor that could give them a medical deferment. American forces in Vietnam were 55% working-class, 25% percent poor, 20% middle-

class. Many soldiers came from rural towns and farming communities.[11]

It is worth noting that many men who received deferments were from wealthy and educated families.

> Prominent political figures accused of avoiding the draft includes Bill Clinton, Joe Biden and Dick Cheney.[12]

This fact about the draft, how young men from the upper classes were able to escape call up, was reflected in some of the prolific antiwar and protest songs of the '60s. In particular, the song 'Fortunate Son' by Creedence Clearwater Revival, released in 1969, dominated the TV and radio stations and was in 'the thoughts of virtually every draft-eligible American male'.[13] It reflected the majority perspective that because they were not 'fortunate sons', they had gone to war or would be drafted soon. The chorus iterating that they weren't the fortunate ones is very heartfelt, and this song was influential in raising awareness to the injustice of the draft.

More significant things about this war need to be highlighted, particularly how it ended, because it has many similarities with what we have experienced today with the war in Afghanistan.

Vietnam Ends in Unnecessary Defeat

In 1972, South Vietnam and the US were winning the war decisively because President Nixon ordered the bombing of military industrial targets in both the capital, Hanoi, and the major port city of Haiphong—in USSR- and Chinese-backed North Vietnam. Nixon would not stop the bombing until North Vietnam attended peace talks in Paris, which they previously abandoned. North Vietnam went back to the peace talks and the bombing was stopped.

During this time, mainstream media—such as ABC, CBS, and the *New York Times* were counter reporting and alarming the American people. A *Washington Post* editorial commented that President Nixon conducted a bombing policy 'so ruthless and so difficult to fathom politically, as to cause millions of Americans to cringe in shame and to wonder at their president's very sanity'.[14] Jane Fonda leading the Hollywood antiwar activism, took a trip to North Vietnam on the invitation of the North Vietnamese delegation to the peace talks in Paris. Although she states it was a 'humanitarian', fact-finding mission, a photo taken of her sitting on an anti-aircraft gun and peering through the sights, and smiling with some North Vietnamese soldiers, did not go down well with the American public, especially American soldiers.

> And other facts about Fonda's trip emerged: Like an updated version of Tokyo Rose, she'd gone on Hanoi radio and petitioned American fighting men stationed to the south to lay down their arms because they were fighting an unjust war against the peace-loving North Vietnamese. She also met with a select group of American POWs – "cooperative" prisoners who'd never shown their captors any resistance – and while those seven have unequivocally stated that they were not coerced to meet with her and tell her all about their fair and humane treatment, other hard-case POWs have said they were tortured before and after her visit.[15]

The Nixon Administration attempted to have Fonda charged with treason, without success; however, she did become the 'most hated woman among Vietnam veterans' and was labelled as 'Hanoi Jane', among other more derogatory names.

On January 27, 1973, President Nixon announced that the Paris Peace Accords had been signed by the US, South Vietnam,

North Vietnam, and the Viet Cong. The American government called it VV Day—Victory in Vietnam Day.

> Later that year, President Nixon abolished the draft and instituted an all-volunteer army. That act largely eviscerated the anti-war movement, which involved millions of draft-age men.[16]

As part of the accord, because the Americans knew that North Vietnam would continue its aggression, they pledged military hardware support to South Vietnam. This promised them piece-by-piece replacements, such as helicopter for helicopter and bullet for bullet, to defend themselves against the north's aggression. These accords were effective in halting the advance of communist tyranny from North Vietnam.

> By August 15, 1973, 95 percent of American troops and their allies had left Vietnam, as well as Cambodia and Laos under the Case-Church Amendment. The amendment, which was approved by the U.S. Congress in June 1973, prohibited further U.S. military activity in those three countries unless the president secured Congressional approval in advance.[17]

But all that had been gained in Vietnam began to fall apart for Nixon after the Watergate scandal and President Nixon's subsequent resignation in August 1974. Vice-President Gerald R. Ford succeeded Nixon, taking the reins of government, but he did not have the support of Democrat-controlled Congress to uphold the promise made to South Vietnam. As North Vietnam was pushing south and taking villages and towns, testing the new US president, South Vietnam was appealing for US support.

On April 10, 1975, President Ford pleaded with Congress in a televised session to the nation to keep the word of the US government to South Vietnam to provide military aid. As Ford delivered his speech, many members stood and walked out. (Interestingly, President Joe Biden was a Democrat senator in Congress at that time.) Since many Democrats (who held the majority vote) had demonstrated years before against the war, and some had either escaped the draft or had sons who received deferment, they were invested in supporting this decision that led to America's failure in Vietnam. This refusal of aid resulted in the surrender of South Vietnam less than three weeks later. This article from the Nixon Foundation explains what happened as a result:

> On April 30, 1975, Saigon's name was changed to Ho Chi Minh City. Within hours, the American Embassy had been ransacked and left in ruins. Up to a million residents were forcibly moved to the countryside. So-called New Economic Zones (NEZ's) and re-education camps were established for "undesirable elements." Executions and other means of sanctioned death were common. In the cities, typewriters were outlawed, and all residents were required to submit to the authorities a list of books they owned and report "all private conversations deemed contrary to the spirit of the revolution."
>
> Estimates of Boat People escapees from the North Vietnamese victors would reach over one million, with 600,000 drowning in the South China Sea.
>
> As for Saigon's one-time ally, the United States, on the night of the surrender of South Vietnam to North Vietnam former Senator J. William Fulbright announced that he was "no more depressed than I would be about Arkansas losing a football game to Texas."[18]

Just two weeks earlier, the communist Khmer Rouge (Communist Party of Kampuchea) were able to take Cambodia, which began a horrendous time of unimaginable cruelty—so much so that the areas of mass killings and executions were named the Killing Fields. Then Laos fell the following December, where they set a record for 'more political prisoners per capita than any other country in the world, including Cambodia and Vietnam'.[19] North Vietnam General Van Tien Dung records in his memoirs that when the US cut their aid to South Vietnam, the president of South Vietnam was 'forced to fight a poor man's war'. In addition, the premier of Cambodia stated, 'We have no more material means' to continue the struggle and 'we feel completely abandoned'.[20]

> The devastation wrought by Indochina's communist movements will stand forever in testimony against the ideological passions of the U.S. antiwar movement as well as those historians who still want their readers to believe the United States was immoral in its attempt to prevent the communists from conquering our allies.[21]

The hippies were very much idealistic. They were rightly angry about the devastation of war, the draft, and the mishandling and underestimation of their nation's involvement in Vietnam. However, they, together with the antiwar movement, failed to understand the degree of evil behind communism or the strategic means needed for successful withdrawal that would provide South Vietnam with the resources to resist the northern takeover.

History Repeats

Fast forward to August 2021. A *Washington Post* article reads:

President Gerald Ford was in a meeting with his energy team when his deputy national security adviser came in and passed him a note. It warned that Saigon was falling, and faster than expected.

Congress and the Pentagon had been pressuring him for weeks to move faster on evacuating Americans and their South Vietnamese allies, and now time was running out.

That's what Ford faced on the evening of April 28, 1975, and it is history repeating itself now.

After 20 years of U.S. involvement, the Taliban seized Afghanistan's capital, Kabul, on Sunday morning, as the United States scrambled to evacuate embassy staff and accelerate the rescue and relocation of Afghans who aided the U.S. military.[22]

The world watched this happen in real time before our eyes. Two wars lost in very similar ways.

Just ten years after the collapse of the Soviet Union under communist Marxist rule, the West entered another long war. On September 11, 2001, the Twin Towers fell. This was the start of the War on Terror that lasted twenty years, ending in Afghanistan much the same way as the Vietnam War. It needn't have. Democratic President Biden took office, an antiwar protester who was both a baby boomer and a 'fortunate son'. He escaped the Vietnam War draft and refused to take the advice of the experienced generals and military advisers. Young soldiers died needlessly. Billions of dollars of valuable military hardware were lost. Thousands of innocent civilians were killed or tortured, or they fled for their lives. Many did not make it. Many went into hiding. All this happened as the door closed and oppressive rule returned.

Like the young boomers, millennials have grown up with a cold war of sorts with the War on Terror. They haven't experienced missiles aimed at them, but they've lived through some fearful times of bombs going off in Western cities and terrorist attacks of crazed gunmen or knife wielding jihadists. Security was ramped up considerably, with airport x-ray machines, bag checking, and extra security staff at airports and events. We got used to the piles of flowers, pictures, candles, and notes left in places where innocents were killed. Children and young people who watched (oftentimes repeatedly) firsthand images and accounts and videos on their social media screens experienced unprecedented anxiety about terrorist attacks. The full impact of emotional stress on millennials may never be known.

Two tragic wars, two tragic and unnecessary outcomes. And at the time of writing, we watch the horrors of the war in Ukraine streamed to our devices.

Young Balladeers Step Up to Articulate the Mood

John Lennon captured the angst of the young idealistic boomers when he sang his popular antiwar song 'Give Peace a Chance'.

The songs that the young people sang have much to reveal about how they were feeling at the time of the Jesus revolution days, as we have already seen with the anti-draft song 'Fortunate Son'.

Barry McGuire released the 1965 hit song 'Eve of Destruction', a popular protest anthem, before his conversion during the Jesus revolution. The song laments the social issues of the time—the Vietnam War, the assassination of John F. Kennedy, the Civil Rights Movement, unrest in the Middle East, the American space program (landing on the moon), and the threat of nuclear war. Some radio stations banned the song because they thought the lyrics were too controversial and said they were 'an aid to the enemy in Vietnam'. The raw emotions expressed in the song of anger, frustration, indignation at hypocrisy, and fear of a sudden missile attack reflected the feelings of the day. The chorus laments that after seeing all that's been happening, still people refused to believe the world was living on the eve of destruction. This was the apocalyptic fear that young people experienced in those tumultuous years, not unlike today.

How the Church Responded to the Vietnam War

So how did the church respond to the Vietnam War? Is there anything to learn that we can apply?

America's involvement in Vietnam divided the Christian community, as have the wars in the Middle East, Afghanistan, and even Ukraine. According to Larry Eskridge, Christians lost an opportunity to reach out to a hurting nation:

> But the Vietnam War was no small matter of debate among American Christians. For many conservative Christians—like evangelist Billy Graham and Francis Cardinal Spellman of New York—the threat of atheistic communism's tyrannical spread inspired ardent support of intensified American involvement in the war. Meanwhile, Clergy and Laity Concerned About Vietnam (CALCAV) and traditional "peace churches" like the Quakers and the Mennonites were key players in the rise of the antiwar movement.
>
> All too often, though, many American Christians simply went about their daily business, virtually ignoring the war until thousands had been killed on both sides. By

that point, stark cultural and political battle lines had been drawn through every segment of American society; for great swaths of the American church a strategic chance to be "salt and light" had passed.[23]

It appears that what we can learn is that the church cannot ignore the issue of wars around the world, whether we are involved or not. This is far more than advocating support for or against war; this is more about recognising the angst of fear, uncertainty, and doubt, and providing hope. And the church cannot do this unless, as Eskridge wisely states, it is salt and light. As we are seeing wars and rumours of wars across the globe, the church must forsake the world and the philosophies of man and radically follow Jesus.

---

1. John Lennon, "Imagine," The Beatles Bible, last updated July 12, 2021, https://www.beatlesbible.com/people/john-lennon/songs/imagine.
2. Larry Eskridge, "Ken Burns's 'The Vietnam War' Is Worth Your Time," The Gospel Coalition, September 22, 2017, https://www.thegospelcoalition.org/article/ken-burns-the-vietnam-war-is-worth-your-time.
3. A great resource for understanding history, and social and cultural issues of today is PragerU. Go to the site and find short 3–5-minute video histories on subjects such as the Cold War, Vietnam War, Korean War, and much more. https://www.prageru.com.
4. Paglia, "Cosmic Consciousness."
5. "Sixties Counterculture: The Hippies and Beyond," *Encyclopedia.com* accessed May 6, 2022, https://www.encyclopedia.com/history/encyclopedias-almanacs-transcripts-and-maps/sixties-counterculture-hippies-and-beyond.
6. Mark Harris, "The Flowering of the Hippies," *Atlantic*, September 1967, https://www.theatlantic.com/magazine/archive/1967/09/the-flowering-of-the-hippies/306619.
7. Andrew Glass, "LBJ accused of hiding Vietnam War's cost, May 18, 1966," *Politico*, May 18, 2015, https://www.politico.com/story/2015/05/this-day-in-politics-may-18-1966-118030.
8. Ibid.
9. Ibid.
10. "Vietnam War Facts, Stats and Myths," US Wings, accessed June 26, 2018, https://www.uswings.com/about-us-wings/vietnam-war-facts.

11. "The Draft and the Vietnam War," Students of History, accessed April 29, 2022, https://www.studentsofhistory.com/vietnam-war-draft.

12. "Military Advancements," Internet Public Library, accessed April 29, 2022, https://www.ipl.org/essay/Military-Advancements-PKG8VPHE28TT.

13. Dave White, "Antiwar protest songs of the '60s and '70s," liveabout, April 12, 2018, https://www.liveabout.com/anti-war-protest-songs-of-the-60s-and-70s-748278.

14. Bruce Herschensohn, "When Night Fell In Indochina," Richard Nixon Foundation, April 30, 2001, https://www.nixonfoundation.org/2001/04/when-night-fell-in-indochina.

15. Ward Carroll, "How Jane Fonda Became the Most-Hated Woman Among Vietnam Veterans," We Are the Mighty, April 2, 2018, https://www.wearethemighty.com/articles/jane-fonda-vietnam.

16. "This week in history: Paris Peace Accords signed, Vietnam War draws down," People's World, January 26, 2018, https://www.peoplesworld.org/article/this-week-in-history-paris-peace-accords-signed-vietnam-war-draws-down.

17. Ibid.

18. Herschensohn, "When Night Fell."

19. Ibid.

20. Ibid.

21. Ibid.

22. Gillian Brockell, "The fall of Saigon: As Taliban seizes Kabul, the Vietnam War's final days remembered," *Washington Post*, August 16, 2021, https://www.washingtonpost.com/history/2021/08/15/saigon-fall-kabul-taliban.

23. Eskridge, "Worth Your Time."

— 13 —

Why Young People Hate Capitalism

This chapter is about how we got to a place where young people are crying out against the injustices of capitalism, the system they see as the root of most of the West's evils and injustices. We've already covered so much of this in other chapters, where the anti-capitalist ideas of Marxism have pervaded much of our education system and our society including the church. Hopefully this chapter will fill in some gaps.

The cultural revolution of the '60s and '70s amongst the young baby boomers, particularly championed by those in universities, wanted to see the end of capitalism as an economic system. These young boomers entered the fields of education, business, and the media, and they have taught their ideas to the next generations over the last decades.

Instead of discarding capitalism completely, many believe it is better to examine why and how capitalism was implemented in the first place and where things have gone wrong. Conserve the good and discard the bad.

My intention also is to help Christians understand and make sense of current economics and the shift we are seeing in large corporations—from simply operating a business to now taking on moral social justice issues that once belonged to the church. What motivated this shift? This chapter will also help explain the narratives that are so prevalent today and promoted by governments and big corporations. In turn, this will help Christians to understand the ideas influencing millennials.

This chapter might be a hard read for those who are not so familiar with the topic, but I have kept things as simple as possible for readers to understand the landscape. I believe it will be very enlightening and relevant. At the end of the chapter, I explain how the church can respond and how it is already responding, in very effective and wonderful ways, to lift society.

For a 'Moral and Religious People'

John Adams (1735–1826), an American founding father, wrote about the American Constitution that it 'was made only for a moral and religious people. It is wholly inadequate to the government of any other'.[1] In other words, the structural foundations of the nation set by the founding fathers in how the government, law, and society would operate would only work if the people were moral and religious, or that most people governed their own consciences. And because most of the New World and founding fathers were theists or Christian in faith, the morality and virtue they aspired to was Judeo-Christian.

Capitalism, the economic system that operates on a free market economy, functions well within a moral and religious society. The government does not regulate or control the market or what is produced (as in socialism and communism). People are free to provide goods and services as they see fit to make a living. If consumers don't like a business's product or service, they won't buy and the business won't prosper. Capitalism is based on human need. We buy what we need or want. 'It encourages people to improve their lives by satisfying the needs of others.'[2] The power is in the hands of the consumer as businesses compete to produce what we need and to the highest quality. There is no other economic system that allows for the poor to move up in the world economically through innovation, creativity, hard work, and perseverance.

The Demise of Capitalism

The main downside to capitalism, of course, is that the sinful heart of man can use this system for exploitation. Consumerism and materialism can dominate and cause the misuse of both people and natural resources. We are now in a post-Christian era when the basic structures of society have been and are being dismantled, and traditional morality and virtue have been abandoned, even mocked. Capitalism today, especially in this post-modern and post-COVID era, is looking more like corporatism.

Corporatism, according to the *Merriam-Webster Dictionary*, is:

> the organization of a society into industrial and professional corporations serving as organs of political representation and exercising control over persons and activities within their jurisdiction.[3]

When the government shutdown smaller businesses during the pandemic, big corporations and businesses prospered. Most sane people can see that something is fundamentally wrong with our economy when, with the government's help, the world's top billionaires multiply their wealth during lockdowns. Big Tech, big pharma, mainstream media, and other 'big' corporations have not only prospered during the pandemic, they are also singing from the same song-sheet. The government ensures that citizens are all hearing the same narrative by keeping dissent at bay through controlling information, cancelling some, and promoting 'independent' fact-checking.

The abandonment of Christian beliefs over the years has meant that capitalism is becoming more exploitative, and young people are noticing. Capitalism's devolution into something like corporatism draws young people to Marxist ideology, perceived as a more equitable system. The impact of the current economic system on young people has been crippling. We already looked at the effect of the mass migration of women into the workforce in the '70s due to the radical women's movement. It changed the economic balance so that nowadays, millennial couples need to both work to maintain a middle-class lifestyle. Helen Andrews laments this phenomenon:

> I realised that millennials are materially disinherited, we are materially well behind what the Baby Boomers had accomplished economically by the time they were our age. So I started investigating that sense that the millennials were not very well off and I discovered that the statistics backed me up. That in terms of wealth accumulation, millennials have accumulated a quarter of what the boomers had when they were our age. Not that we're 75% of where the boomers are right now, we're 75% behind where they were when they were in their 20s and 30s. So I tried to trace back where all of these fears of society had gone wrong. What happened to destroy our churches, what happened to destroy our families and our schools and our economy? And every single thread that I pulled on led me back to the same place; the generation that came of age in the 1960s, and was shaped by the 1960s, and then attained the summits of power in the 1990s—the Baby Boomers. They were behind all the decline that I investigated.[4]

According to Andrews, the baby boomers made a huge impact and still influence the world, but future generations will suffer if they don't correct course.

But back to understanding a bit more about corporatism and how it's influencing governments around the world. It's important to briefly cover the World Economic Forum (WEF). This organisation is a major player today, and we must understand its objectives because it aims to change the current capitalist economic system of the West, and giant corporations are both members and advocates.

Interestingly, the WEF began in the counter-culture '70s.

The World Economic Forum

In 1971, a German by the name of Klaus Schwab founded the WEF. It grew to be a leading global think tank for governments on policies ranging from tax to the environment. They hold annual meetings our government representatives attend with the purpose of gleaning ideas to take back to their countries and implement. In addition, major corporations are also partners and take on their ideas to implement. The WEF is connected to influential individuals such as Bill Gates and George Soros, as well as celebrities and climate change personalities.

Klaus Schwab created the WEF in 1971 because he believed that the West needed a new economic system. He wrote in a 2019 *Time* magazine article that when 'shareholder capitalism … first gained ground in the United States in the 1970s, and expanded its influence globally in the following decades … hundreds of millions of people around the world prospered, as profit seeking companies unlocked new markets and created new jobs'.[5] Regardless of this, in 1971, Schwab wanted to influence world leaders to implement a new kind of capitalism—what he described as 'more virtuous' and encouraged us to 'reimagine capitalism'. He believed that shareholder capitalism had failed because of reasons to do with equity, environmental issues, and inclusivity.

As stated, the WEF not only influences leaders of nations; they also influence giant corporation partners who have a seat at their table. Klaus Schwab does not agree with the free market notion that 'business of business is business', meaning that businesses are there to provide a service or product and make profit for their shareholders, create jobs, and so on. Schwab believes that a *more virtuous* economic system is possible, saying, 'Rather than chasing short-term profits or narrow self-interest, companies could pursue the well-being of all people and the entire planet.'[6]

To do this, the WEF is proposing that large businesses and governments work together for the global good of the planet. Hence, we see today that major banks, telecommunications, media corporations, airlines, shipping companies, pharmaceutical companies, Big Tech, and so on have taken on social justice issues such as climate change, environmentalism, LGBQ+ issues, BLM goals, diversity inroads, and feminist agenda issues. (A full list of WEF partners can be found on their website, as well as their agendas—which appear to predominantly focus on environmental issues.)

For example, BlackRock company, a WEF partner and 'the world's biggest asset manager, recently passing $10 trillion in assets', has been accused of going 'woke' and mandating all sorts of employee training in social justice ideology.[7]

The world's most powerful investor told CEOs not to worry about coming off as woke.

> Larry Fink, the founder, chairman and boss of BlackRock, has told company chiefs to embrace "stakeholder capitalism" - the growing vogue in business for balancing the need for profits against other concerns such as worker welfare and impact on the planet.
>
> "Stakeholder capitalism is not about politics. It is not a social or ideological agenda. It is not 'woke,'" Fink

wrote in his annual letter to CEOs. "It is capitalism, driven by mutually beneficial relationships between you and the employees, customers, suppliers, and communities your company relies on to prosper. This is the power of capitalism."[8]

It's not the power of capitalism, it is the power of corporatism. Giant companies have taken over from the church as the moral regulators of society.

From ANZ bank's ad a number of years back—featuring little girls repeating the inequities of the debunked gender wage gap myth—to the Telstra ads today—featuring two children counting trees and writing notes about the 'evil' capitalist workers marking trees to be felled for development—big corporations have indeed become woke. They are no longer just providing a service or product; they are also 'improving the state of the world' by giving us global citizens our pep talks about morality and what is 'more virtuous'. Klaus Schwab writes that this aspect of improving the state of the world should be the ultimate purpose of large companies.[9]

The *Dallas Morning News* wrote an insightful article that illustrates this point:

> A billboard in London recently featured a bizarre advertisement for the multinational bank HSBC. It depicted an androgynous person applying mascara and a bold message: "Gender's just too fluid for borders."
>
> HSBC would seem to have no business interest in gender theory, except that the bank, too, rejects borders. The bank lobbied aggressively against Brexit in 2016 and has protested the result ever since. The free flow of capital brooks no constraints.

The same goes for much of corporate behavior today. On this side of the pond, major corporations have aligned themselves publicly with progressive political and social causes, from LGBTQ+ pride and abortion rights to racial justice and climate change. American business long served as the archetypal bourgeois institution: meritocratic, buttoned-up, and reliably Republican.[10]

In addition, we now see that where the mainstream media (MSM) corporations once held governments to account, many now align themselves to the same message as the government and big corporations; they all appear to sit at the one table. As a result, scores of people seek other independent sources for news that do not repeat the mind-numbing propaganda of 'This is what you need to think and believe'. Independent media is fast outgrowing mainstream media viewing. In an article titled 'Independent News Is Crushing Mainstream Media', Katherine Strange concludes:

> In the face of the MSM's irrational attacks on independent journalists, some of the most credible voices are moving to their own platforms, and finding success. Not only that, but liberals and conservatives are finding common ground in defending and championing free speech — and the independent media sources and voices who bring it to them.[11]

As a result of this explosion in independent media and news sources, Big Tech platforms such as Google, YouTube, Facebook, Twitter, Instagram, and the like have moved to become regulators or news police who can shut down anyone who doesn't sing from the 'more virtuous', woke song-sheet. An eruption of 'independent fact-checkers' work hard for our global good to ensure we receive the 'correct' information, which is to follow the narrative. And as we do our shopping, we are comforted by the repeated calming message to be responsible as 'we are all in this together'.

Klaus Schwab concluded in a *Time* article that if businesses 'really want to leave their mark on the world, there is no alternative' than to work towards bringing 'the world closer to achieving shared goals'.[12] And that is looking more like a corporatism model, and ominously like fascism—where government or the state and state-directed big business work together, as was the Nationalist *Socialist* German Workers Party known as the Nazis. Unlike what we have been led to believe, fascism is actually a form of socialism based on Marxist ideas.

Schwab proposes that the finance system of the world needs a readjustment, therefore the WEF promotes this in the form of The Great Reset. It's not a conspiracy theory, it's an openly discussed and promoted initiative of the WEF. On their website they announce, 'There is an urgent need for global stakeholders [not shareholders] to cooperate in simultaneously managing the direct consequences of the COVID-19 crisis. To improve the state of the world, the World Economic Forum is starting The Great Reset initiative.'[13] As they expressed, it will be 'more virtuous' for the greater good of all people globally.

But what is 'virtue' without truth?

Late Capitalism

As discussed, the capitalist system works well in a moral and religious society. In our post-Christian modern world, we see some concerning evidence of the uncompassionate and inhumane aspects of capitalism rising to prominence. Big corporations cleverly mask their shallowness in outwardly virtue signalling social justice issues. 'Late capitalism' is a term we now commonly hear; however, it was a phrase coined by European economists back around the Second World War. The socialist Frankfurt School academics were concerned that late capitalism might stifle the working class's potential for revolution.[14] They concluded that people should not love the benefits of a free market economy too much.

Capitalism without Christian virtue has turned into a tireless frenzy of materialism, consumerism, and marketing driven by profit and greed and dominated by big corporations. There are always products that will improve our lives that we must have.

The skyrocketing housing market is a classic example of something gone terribly wrong with our economy. Many people, especially the young, are seemingly barred from the American or Aussie dream of owning their own home. Douglas Murray, author of the *Sunday Times* best seller *The Madness of Crowds: Gender, Race and Identity*, highlights why he believes young people are attracted to the Marxist ideas of wokism:

> Although the foundations had been laid for several decades, it is only since the financial crash of 2008 that there has been a march into the mainstream of ideas that were previously known solely on the obscurest fringes of academia. The attractions of this new set of beliefs are obvious enough. It is not clear why a generation which can't accumulate capital should have any great love of capitalism. Likewise it isn't hard to work out why a generation who believe they may never own a home could be attracted to an ideological world view that promises to sort out every inequity, not just in their own lives but every inequity on earth.[15]

This ideology is a philosophy of man. It explains what has gone wrong (oppression) and how to fix it (fight oppression).

As giant corporations, that is big businesses, enjoy the capitalist system and promote social justice causes, they promote their 'virtue' in order to retain and gain customers and build their clientele. Their efforts appear to exonerate themselves before the world rather than to genuinely fight a just cause.

As for big companies, how many of them use cheap labour in Asia, where phenomenal human rights abuses exist? Factories with poor working conditions, child labourers, and women working long and crippling hours are not a concern, unless, of course, companies are found out.

With late capitalism, 'progressive values are now a powerful branding tool'.[16] Since corporations are after profits, they overlook any social issue that needs genuine reform. Corporations don't have morals. Even stakeholder capitalism, aka corporatism, is really just about money and influence. In an article titled 'How Capitalism Drives Cancel Culture', we see the underlying motivations behind corporations' wokism:

> But we should be aware of the economic incentives here, particularly given the speed of social media, which can send a video viral, and see onlookers demand a response, before the basic facts have been established. Afraid of the reputational damage that can be incurred in minutes, companies are behaving in ways that range from thoughtless and uncaring to sadistic.[17]

We see this happen before our eyes as people lose their jobs and are publicly disgraced for voicing a personal opinion on social media if it does not align with the accepted woke narrative.

Young people perceive that the contemporary capitalist system is not working and is downright corrupt because the rich are just getting richer. It's like playing a game of Monopoly—the big cheaters keep winning. It's obvious to all, and after appealing to the pertinent authority, we find out that they'll either do nothing or might even be benefitting from or assisting the cheaters. (This is called crony capitalism—where businesses and government have too close a relationship. The government or state puts regulations and restrictions on the competition of the big players, who then funnel money into election campaigns.)

We watch the news and see the protests of young people yelling 'Tax the rich!' as this seems like the only thing to bring equity. And big corporations, celebrities, elites, and progressive politicians echo 'Tax the rich!' as they profit from wokeness and the propaganda that MSM feeds us.

The only economic alternative offered to young people is the Marxist ideas that have been cleverly packaged and delivered through the education system and promoted by celebrities.

Artificial Intelligence Provides Hope for Young People

Besides socialism, young people now put their hope in the prospect of artificial intelligence (AI) to implement justice and equity because AI is not corrupt, or is it?

The World Economic Forum's 'Millennial Manifesto' preaches this message to our global young people. Millennials hold more faith in a system of governance run by artificial intelligence than by fellow human beings who can be corrupted. AI technology can hold information about citizens, monitor citizens, control citizens, make major decisions about citizens and even provide them with a social credit score for being *good* citizens. And that measurement of social credit will be based on whoever has the power to decide what is good and what is not.

> More young people hold faith in governance by a system of artificial intelligence than by a fellow human being. Yet, we need to use these most human and community-

> centered principles as a compass when navigating the complex paths ahead …
>
> To mount the response required to usher in this new world, the Millennial Manifesto team - a component of the Davos Lab - held dialogues on what a matured form of youth activism could look like. Through a process that engaged diverse Global Shapers from every continent, some of the world's most impactful social entrepreneurs, and experienced grassroots activists, the purpose of the dialogues was to devise principles to guide young people as they advocate for a more inclusive post-COVID period. [18]

As millennials lead us forward, we desperately hope they will not fall into the category of those who forget history because for sure, they are bound to repeat it.

A Biblical Response

Gradually, but particularly accelerated since the '60s and '70s, the West lost the grand narrative of why we are here and what our purpose is. As Solzhenitsyn said of the Russian 'ruinous revolution that swallowed up 60 million of our people', 'men have forgotten God; that's why all this has happened'.[19] Douglas Murray, who does not profess to be a Christian but claims to be a 'believer in belief' affirms that this is what is happening in the West too:

> People in wealthy Western democracies today could not simply remain the first people in recorded history to have absolutely no explanation for what we are doing here, and no story to give life purpose. Whatever else they lacked, the grand narratives of the past at least gave life meaning. The question of what exactly we are meant

> to do now – other than get rich where we can and have whatever fun is on offer – was going to have to be answered by something.[20]

The grand narrative is entrusted to God's people to demonstrate and exhibit before the world the purpose and meaning of life. We must not lose our saltiness through absorbing the empty philosophies the world offers, particularly those philosophies that claim to solve humanity's problems apart from God.

As to the economic system and finance, the church must understand the biblical world view regarding finance. It is to be used for 'social good, specifically for stewardship, justice, and love'.[21]

> Stewardship is obedience to God's mandate to increase his creation from something like a garden to something like a city, all the while remembering it is his. We are to care for it and we will be held accountable as stewards. Justice is treating persons with due respect for their rights as humans, these rights based on the fact that every human is loved by God. Love is caring for another person by seeking to bring about their flourishing as an end in itself, and with due respect for that person as a human. Finance within this framework is an excellent place for a Christian to work and to seek societal renewal and transformation, despite the pervasive impact of sin in finance.[22]

Over the centuries, we have seen the work of Christians who led the way in social welfare and reform, from hospitals and schools to movements such as anti-slavery abolitionists and the Royal Society for the Prevention of Cruelty to Animals (RSPCA). These social reforms were funded and led by Christians, incredible thinkers of the time from mixed backgrounds like business, politics, inventing, teaching, farming, science, and craftsmanship.

From the early church to today, Christians have cared for the poor, the sick, and the down and out. The welfare state has taken over much of the work of Christian charities, with many of them, such as hospitals and organisations for youth and homeless people, eventually becoming government-run entities or heavily dependent on government funding—and therefore separated from their Christian mission. They have become beholden to the government's philosophy on care, which is hostile to the Christian gospel. Even Christian schools must teach the Marxist critical theory ideas, although they are packaged in nice-sounding and inarguable terms such as equity, diversity, anti-bullying, and social justice.

Christians continue to lead the fight against abortion, which began with the Roe vs Wade ruling in 1973 that opened the floodgates to the abortion pandemic. This is one of the greatest social justice issues of our time, with 73 million induced abortions per year across the world.[23] That's over three times the population of Australia each year. Protecting the rights of the voiceless and most vulnerable of our society is not unlike the abolitionist movement goals, in a time when most people were indifferent to the cruelty and inhumanity of the slave trade and the buying and selling of priceless souls.

In addition, a renewal is happening amongst churches across the world in that they are moving back to seeking the welfare of their cities and communities. Movement.org, and its initiative Movement Day, is one such network that sees a phenomenal impact across many nations. Their mission is to unite leaders in a town or city—of churches, nonprofits, marketplaces, and local government—to work together to solve the spiritual, physical, and social needs of their cities.[24] Bringing the Christian community together, they first commit themselves to prayer and submission to unity and then seek to discover how to promote the welfare of the people:

> Whether it's as basic as online population, employment, academic performance and immigration research, or as sophisticated as hiring professionals to gather detailed and granular research on a community, city or region, good research compels action.
>
> We have discovered that the average leader in the average church has little idea of what is actually happening in their city. Armed with compelling research, the informed church can rally around common challenges and establish powerful agreement on what needs to be done as well as what they can accomplish together.[25]

The impact of these groups is significant, from beautifying ugly and desolate areas of cities to establishing parks and gardens to setting up relief initiatives for the poor and unemployed. They provide employment and training, get people back on their feet, and support families in need. They believe that real social flourishing involves spiritual renewal, and they are gospel motivated.

Christians are making a difference and now, more than ever, the body of Christ must show what true virtue looks like.

> *'But seek the welfare of the city where I have sent you into exile, and pray to the Lord on its behalf, for in its welfare you will find your welfare' (Jeremiah 29:7).*

1. John Adams, "From John Adams to Massachusetts Militia, 11 October 1798," National Archives, Founder Online, accessed May 16, 2022, https://founders.archives.gov/documents/Adams/99-02-02-3102
2. PragerU, "Capitalism vs Socialism," uploaded March 4, 2019, YouTube video, 5:28, https://www.youtube.com/watch?v=Fdfru9NHGvE.
3. *Merriam-Webster.com Dictionary*, s.v. "corporatism," accessed May 6, 2022, https://www.merriam-webster.com/dictionary/corporatism.
4. Stuckey, "Blaming Boomers."
5. Klaus Schwab, "What Kind of Capitalism Do We Want?" *Time*, December 2, 2019, https://time.com/5742066/klaus-schwab-stakeholder-capitalism-davos.
6. Klaus Schwab, "A Better Economy Is Possible. But We Need to Reimagine Capitalism to Do It," *Time*, October 2020, https://time.com/collection/great-reset/5900748/klaus-schwab-capitalism.
7. Oscar Williams-Grut, "BlackRock CEO Larry Fink tells bosses: Don't listen to critics who say you're 'woke'," Yahoo Lifestyle, republished from the *Evening Standard*, January 18, 2022, https://au.lifestyle.yahoo.com/blackrock-ceo-larry-fink-tells-103639620.html.
8. Ibid.
9. Schwab, "Better Economy."
10. Wells King, "Woke capitalism is a smokescreen," American Compass, republished from the *Dallas Morning News*, December 19, 2021, https://americancompass.org/articles/woke-capitalism-is-a-smokescreen.
11. Katherine Strange, "Independent News is Crushing the Mainstream Media," *Conejo Guardian*, July 20, 2021, https://www.conejoguardian.org/2021/07/20/independent-news-is-crushing-the-mainstream-media.
12. Schwab, "Davos' Klaus Schwab."
13. "The Great Reset," World Economic Forum, accessed February 11, 2022, https://www.weforum.org/great-reset.
14. Patrick Hollis, "Late Capitalism: How it is present in the 21st century," *Medium*, September 30, 2019, https://pjhollis123.medium.com/late-capitalism-d946af4ddc22.
15. Douglas Murray, "Crowds running us over a cliff," *Daily Declaration*, September 14, 2019, https://blog.canberradeclaration.org.au/2019/09/14/crowds-running-us-over-a-cliff.
16. Helen Lewis, "How Capitalism Drives Cancel Culture," *Atlantic*, July 14, 2020, https://www.theatlantic.com/international/archive/2020/07/cancel-culture-and-problem-woke-capitalism/614086.
17. Ibid.
18. "The 'Millennial Manifesto' outlines principles for an inclusive future," World Economic Forum, August 17, 2021, https://www.weforum.org/agenda/2021/08/the-millennial-manifesto-outlines-principles-for-an-inclusive-future.
19. Solzhenitsyn, "Solzhenitsyn's Speech."
20. Douglas Murray, *The Madness of Crowds: Gender, Race and Identity* (London: Bloomsbury Publishing plc, 2020), chapter introduction.

21. TOW Project, "What Does the Bible Say About Finance? (Overview)," Theology of Work, accessed February 15, 2022, https://www.theologyofwork.org/key-topics/finance.

22. Ibid.

23. "Abortion Rates by Country 2022," World Population Review, accessed February 15, 2022, https://worldpopulationreview.com/country-rankings/abortion-rates-by-country.

24. "Today's Cities Are Facing Critical Challenges," Movement Day, accessed February 16, 2022, https://www.movementday.com.

25. "Our Mission," Movement.org, accessed February 16, 2022, https://www.movement.org/our-mission.

— 14 —

The Family and Church

Billy Graham's evaluation was spot on when he said that the vast majority of young people during the tumultuous '60s and '70s counter-culture were still alienated, uncommitted, and uninvolved. The young people he was speaking of were, of course, the baby boomer generation.

To iterate, many young people today look around and see that things are not right, particularly with:

- the rapidly changing woke issues,
- the absence of objective truth,
- the lack of purpose,
- gender confusion,
- feminism, and
- the decimation of marriage, the family, and other structures of society.

They find that they need to reorientate themselves to navigate their way forward. The trend of young people looking into the more traditional orthodox churches is just one example of their seeking stability and structure.[1] Another would be the huge numbers of young people, especially young men, following father figures (like Jordan Peterson) or the many conservative voices on social media (who advocate Judeo-Christian principles), as I wrote about in my previous book *Lost Boys: Bring them home*.

It's obvious that Christianity is in decline in the West. We see this not just by looking at census data, but by firsthand observation. Scores of churches are filled with elderly people. There are few young families, children, or youth, and churches continually struggle to bring in young people and keep them from falling away.

We've looked at society in general, but why do we see the decline in Christianity since the Jesus revolution that saw the conversion of thousands upon thousands?

In this chapter, I cover two fundamental, God-given institutions that suffered a major blow over the decades: the family and the church. The attack on these two God-ordained institutions has been subtle and lethal, but not unrecoverable. By looking at what I see as one of the most lethal methods of attack on families and the church, we can, by the grace of God, resist, take hold of what we have, and rebuild these extraordinary and life-giving institutions for the sake of our children.

The God of *Self*

Theologian and author Thaddeus Williams claims that the fastest-growing religion in the world is the cult of self-worship.[2] I agree. I first learned about the innate human propensity to selfishness through raising five children. Amongst the first essential words of a baby's vocabulary were the one-syllable commands of 'Mine!' and 'No!' Contrary to popular belief, children don't have to learn to be selfish; they are born that way. They have to *learn* to be good. That means learning how to share and look out for others—or to deny self.

The Bible is replete with instruction on training and disciplining children, but it appears to be a lost skill in many Christian families and in Western society at large.

Parenting is all about protection, affection and direction.[3] It involves taming of the defiant, narcissistic self. It must be dethroned or else it will rule like a tyrant.

Psychology Usurps the Bible

Even though many people may not have heard of Doctor Benjamin Spock (1903–1998)—no, he is not the *Star Trek* character—he had an incredible influence on our culture. Spock wrote a book the year after World War II ended called *The Common Sense Book of Baby and Child Care*, and it took off like wildfire, with subsequent updated versions. It's listed as one of the most sold non-fiction books of all time.[4] Spock was even named in *LIFE* magazine as among the hundred most important Americans of the 20th century. Being a doctor meant that his advice was sound. Or was it? An article on Family Ministries website, 'How Dr. Spock Is Destroying America', explains what happened under Spock's instruction:

> Instead of stressing the importance of teaching self-denial and respect for authority, Spock emphasized accommodating children's feelings and catering to their preferences. No longer did children learn they could endure Brussels sprouts and suffer through daily chores. Using Spock's approach, parents began to feed self-indulgence instead of instilling self-control – homes were becoming less parent-directed and more child-centered. As parents elevated children's "freedom of expression" and natural cravings, children became more outspoken, defiant, and demanding of gratification. In fact, they came to view gratification as a "right."[5]

Doctor Spock promoted what is known as permissive parenting—putting low demands on kids coupled with a lot of attention and responsiveness from parents. Or simply put, enforcing very little structure and control. It is sometimes referred to as 'indulgent or passive parenting'.⁶ Indulgent parents operate on feelings to inform them how to respond to children's behaviour. We have all witnessed indulgent or permissive parenting and cannot but feel sorry for the parents.

> Even Dr. Spock was aware of his negative influence upon parents. In a 1968 interview with the New York Times, Spock admitted that his first edition of "Common Sense Book of Baby and Child Care" contributed to an increase of permissive parenting in America. "Parents began to be afraid to impose on the child in any way," he said. In his 1957 edition, he tried to remedy that by emphasizing the need for setting standards and asking for respect. Unfortunately, Spock failed to see the deeper problems of his philosophy, so subsequent editions continued to cultivate narcissism.⁷

Interestingly, Spock was politically active during the '60s and '70s. He participated in anti-Vietnam War demonstrations and was even found guilty of plotting to aid those wanting to avoid the draft—a ruling that was appealed and later cancelled. In 1972, Spock ran as a presidential candidate of the United States for the socialist People's Party. This point is significant because it reveals the origin of Spock's ideas that challenged the authority of parents over their children.

Doctor Spock changed the definition of parental love to mean *indulgence* and *to rescue children from challenges, deprivation, and the consequences of their actions*.⁸ As we have progressed over the last fifty years, society has looked more and more to the 'experts'—the psychologists—as authorities on how to raise our children.

Christian psychologist, author, and parent guru John Rosemond writes scathingly about his own profession.

They, psychologists and mental health professionals by other titles, don't know what they are talking about when it comes to children, parenting, families, and people in general. And they refuse to admit it ...

About human beings, the Bible tells us one thing, psychology tells us something else entirely. The Bible says, for example, that high esteem for oneself is bad mojo. Psychology says bad mojo is good mojo. The Bible says that the gospel is sufficient to heal whatever ails you, mental or physical. Psychology says psychology is not just sufficient but absolutely necessary, along with drugs that have never reliably outperformed placebos in clinical trials (NONE OF THEM!) to heal whatever ails your mental state. How can a biblical worldview be reconciled with psychology when they obviously exist in a state of philosophical incompatibility? In a word: Can't.

Do today's parents raise children the way parents in the 1950s raised children? No. Today's parents raise children according to bogus psychological theory. Their grandparents raised children according to biblical principle, tradition, and common-sense. Has child mental health improved since the 1950s? No, it is at least ten times worse. Does 1 and 1 make 2? Yes, unless one is a victim of public-school math, in which case 1 and 1 make whatever you need it to make to continue feeling special.

Psychology has not improved the lot of any group of American citizens except psychologists, who have successfully convinced most American citizens that they know what they're doing when it comes to kids, parents, families, and humans in general. Because of their success at promoting the myth of psychology, psychologists generally make a lot of money. It is relevant to note that most of them are atheists ... Psychologists are con artists.⁹

Don't miss Rosemond's point that psychology and a biblical world view are opposites when it comes to advice on child training. (Please note, I am not for or against psychology in this book; my aim is to help readers consider where psychology might undermine or replace biblical teaching and biblical order.)

We have a God-given responsibility to train up our children in righteousness. It is a wonderful and demanding responsibility, and we can do it! The body of Christ can work together so that those who are gifted in godly parenting can teach others. The example of respectful, happy, and obedient children is an outstanding testimony to the world.

Discipleship Deficit

Not only has there been a Christian parenting crisis, but there has been a discipleship deficit too, perhaps one that has led on from permissive parenting. The seeker-friendly churches that took off in the '70s were most likely an over-adjustment to the seemingly stoic and serious church environment that new seekers could not relate to. It became important to appeal to the unchurched. Creating seeker-friendly churches included having relatable music styles and more casual clothing. This meant removing religious icons like crosses from steeples or sanctuaries, or removing communion from Sunday services. In conscious efforts to avoid offending seekers, sermons tended to be motivational talks with man-centred messages. Other aspects to create a seeker-friendly environment included the use of videos, music, drama, and other forms of art—ideas borrowed from secular marketing for the purpose of evangelism.

To unpack what is meant by man-centred sermons and messages, Pastor Matt Chandler explains that this is 'a way of reading the Bible that makes man the hero and not the acts of God'.[10] He says that the Bible consistently wants to take our eyes off ourselves and put them onto a God who is able. The account of David and Goliath reflects this.

In an excerpt from the movie *American Gospel*, Chandler uses the account of David and Goliath as a perfect example of God as our hero. He explains that with man-centred sermons, preachers talk about us as being David with Goliath representing our huge problem, whether it's financial, relational, traumatic, or whatever. It's a narcissistic way to read the Bible. Instead, Chandler says that in a Christ-centred hermeneutic, we see that within this story there is something terrifying that cannot be defeated, yet it is overcome by a mere boy, 'who, by faith, killed what couldn't be killed'. David faced the enemies of God for the victory and salvation of God's people. Christ conquers our giants; we don't. 'What's more undefeatable than sin and death?'[11]

Michael Stafford, in a 2013 article, wrote:

> Like an enormous object in space, the Cult of the Self also exerts an enormous cultural gravitational pull that distorts Christian belief and practice in America, and is a non-Christian belief system that has given rise to Christian heresies. Under this system, Jesus is a tame toothless bourgeoisie moraliser who demands nothing of us; God is relegated to the position of a life coach, an investment adviser, or worse, a cosmic bookie. This is particularly obvious in the heresies of the so-called

> "prosperity gospel" where Christianity is, in the words of Bell, "about meeting our wildest consumer dreams."[12]

We Christians must remind ourselves that the chief purpose of the church is the gathering of God's people to worship, equip the saints for ministry, and build up the body of Christ (Ephesians 4:11–12).

Many churches keep their teaching at a very shallow level, perhaps more so for what attendees want to hear than what they need to hear. In man-centred Christian practice, man can apply his own individual interpretation to Scripture. Parishioners become consumers and can shop elsewhere if they don't like the experience. The seeker-friendly church is full of perpetual babes in Christ (or still to be converted members) who are fed on milk and *entertained* every Sunday. Stafford continues:

> In addition, traditional Christian beliefs and teachings, particularly regarding human sexuality and marriage, are stripped away lest they impose limitations on the desires of autonomous selves as we increasingly adopt a "cafeteria" style approach to religious belief, picking and choosing among doctrines and practices like customers sampling a buffet.
>
> Through these processes, Christianity is rendered impotent and unable to critique either consumerism, capitalism, or our libertine social mores.[13]

The more traditional churches have not had much success in discipling their youth and new converts either. Despite the same ritualistic practices in services, one hour each week is not enough to teach and train young people while they are simultaneously being trained and indoctrinated by the world around them.

The Next Revolution

Timothy Keller wrote a small book called *How to Reach the West Again*,[14] which provides insight into how to fortify our young people and new converts by thoroughly teaching the tenants of the Christian faith through the catechism—a book that teaches biblical truth in an orderly way. In essence, it consists of a series of questions, like:

- What is the chief purpose of man?
- What is God?
- How do we glorify God?
- How do we know there is a God?
- What is the Word of God?
- How do we know that the Bible is the Word of God?
- Are there more gods than one?
- What are the decrees or eternal purposes of God?

It's hard to imagine that children in the past learned the answers to these questions and the Scriptures that support the doctrine.

Keller explains that many years ago, Sunday schools abandoned the teaching of the catechism in favour of shallow Bible stories. The early church and the church during the Reformation used this same method of catechesis or religious instruction, and it was used in most churches up until perhaps fifty years ago. Keller believes that the catechism (there are a few of them, including the Westminster Catechism) needs to be updated to counter the prevailing secular beliefs of today.[15]

Methodical and disciplined instruction on the catechism (not unlike learning mathematical tables or spelling) would arm young Christians with the ability to recognise and soundly refute the world's secular narratives. These come at them now dozens of times a day—or even per hour—in ads, tweets, music, movies, stories, opinion pieces, etc. And these narratives sound good because they are mixed with truth and they are self-gratifying.

Keller identifies some common narratives such as these:

> You have to be true to yourself.
>
> You should be free to live as you choose, as long as you don't hurt anyone.
>
> You must do what makes you happiest. You can't sacrifice that for anyone.
>
> Everyone has the right to decide what is right and wrong themselves.[16]

How does a young person with a kindergarten level of biblical knowledge refute these narratives with biblical truth?

Jeremy Boreing, a Christian social commentator, said it well about the poorly discipled young Christians today:

> When you teach your children only caricatures of the arguments against your own position, you send them into battle worse than unarmed. You send them into battle against mechanized armies with wooden swords painted silver. And they think they are actually armed, and then they get out in the world and they hear actual smart arguments against what they believe, and they crumble. And when they crumble, they believe what my parents taught me is a lie because they led me like a sheep unto the slaughter.[17]

The Fastest-Growing Religion

After examining the philosophy of Doctor Spock and his permissive parenting, and the subsequent departure from biblical parenting by Christians, and the need for churches to address the discipleship deficit, we can see why young people struggle. Thaddeus Williams, in his article 'Self-Worship Is the World's Fastest-Growing Religion' (and the world's oldest religion—Genesis 3), lays out some disturbing statistics:

> 84 percent of Americans believe that "enjoying yourself is the highest goal of life."
>
> Further, 86 percent believe that to enjoy yourself you must "pursue the things you desire most."
>
> And 91 percent affirm this statement: "To find yourself, look within yourself."[18]

Williams believes that the answer to the very first question in the Westminster Catechism—What is the chief end of man?—has been inverted. How so? The answer is: The chief end of man is to glorify God and enjoy Him forever, but Williams rewrites it for today's generation: The chief end of man is to glorify and enjoy *himself* forever.[19]

Williams succinctly explains why the cult of self-worship leads to shipwrecked lives:

> Here's the problem with this cult of self-worship—besides the obvious problem of being a rebellion against God: When we try to be our own sources of truth, we slowly drive ourselves crazy. When we try to be our own sources of satisfaction, we become miserable wrecks. When we become our own standard of goodness and justice, we become obnoxiously self-righteous. When we seek self-glorification, we become more inglorious.
>
> Why? It's simple. We are not God. We were never meant to trust in or be defined by, satisfied in, and captivated by ourselves. We were made to revere someone infinitely more interesting and awesome than

ourselves. We become most truly and freely ourselves in a state of self-forgetful reverence. As Albert Einstein put it, "A person first starts to live when he can live outside himself."

The more self-absorbed we are, the less awe we experience; the less awe we experience, the less fully and freely ourselves we become.[20]

Aleksandr Solzhenitsyn wrote about what he learned when imprisoned in the Russian gulags:

Meeting these hidden heroes [those who suffered in the gulags] started a revolution against the greatest totalitarian ruler of all: myself.[21]

Yes, self is the greatest totalitarian and oppressive ruler of all, and it can never lead us to freedom.

What the Church Must Do to Resist Selfism

The world has indeed converted the church to selfism ever so subtly, but as I mentioned at the start of the chapter, it is not unrecoverable. Our maker provides us with everything that leads to life and godliness, including instructions on how to raise and build flourishing families, churches, and communities. In addition, we are given the Holy Spirit to guide us and empower us to expand the kingdom of God as His image bearers.

Stafford also provides practical directions for the church:

In practical terms, ... we must form and sustain communities of table fellowship, both physical and virtual, conducive to authentic human flourishing that are incubators of virtue. This can take diverse shapes and forms and at a minimum it must involve dethroning the desire for fame and fortune from its present primacy; fostering vertical solidarity between rich and poor as well as horizontal solidarity between consumers and producers; rendering effective assistance to marginalised groups in society, and any brothers and sisters within the community who may be in need; a shared commitment to traditional values, particularly with respect to sex and marriage, as well as a recognition of the importance of families and children to the life of the community; opposition to abortion; an emphasis on environmental stewardship and caring for creation; nonviolence; submission to compassionate correction by the community and legitimate religious authority; forgiveness; hospitality to strangers; and recognition of the importance of prayer and its central role in daily life.[22]

In chapter 16 and 17, I unpack what Christianity looked like in the early church times, during the communist atheist regime, and how it looks in the persecuted church today. All of these are examples of the church as the counter-culture—not being converted by the pagan or secular world, that looks inward to self, but resisting the world and converting the lost. Christians *in* the world but not *of* the world.

But before that, it will be to our advantage to look at today's young generation Z, which is the most impacted by the philosophy of selfism and the dismantling of the basic structures that provide stability and meaning for society.

---

1. Sparks, "Young People."

2. Thaddeus Williams, "Self-Worship Is the World's Fastest-Growing Religion," The Gospel Coalition, November 10, 2021, https://www.thegospelcoalition.org/article/self-worship-booms.

3. John Rosemond, *John Rosemond's New Parent Power!* (Kansas City, Missouri: Andrews McMeel Publishing, 2001).

4. Paula Fass, "There Used to Be a Consensus on How to Raise Kids," *Atlantic*, March 2018, https://www.theatlantic.com/family/archive/2018/03/america-new-dr-spock/555311.

5. "How Dr. Spock is Destroying America," Family Ministries, accessed January 10, 2022, http://www.familyministries.com/dr_spock.htm.

6. Emily Guarnotta, "Permissive Parenting: Definition, Characteristics, & Effectiveness," Choosing Therapy, updated April 5, 2022, https://www.choosingtherapy.com/permissive-parenting.

7. WND Staff, "How Dr. Spock destroyed America," WND, January 27, 2009, https://www.wnd.com/2009/01/87179.

8. Family Ministries, "Dr. Spock."

9. John Rosemond, "Old Fashioned Child Rearing Is Where It's At," John Rosemond, September 2, 2021, https://www.rosemond.com/Old-Fashioned-Child-Rearing-Is-Where-It-s-At.html.

10. American Gospel, "American Gospel: Christ Alone (1 Hour Version)," uploaded March 11, 2019, YouTube video, 58:33, https://www.youtube.com/watch?v=ocHm18wUAGU.

11. Ibid.

12. Stafford, "Christian resistance.'"

13. Ibid.

14. Tim Keller, *How to Reach the West Again: Six Essential Elements of a Missionary Encounter*, (New York City: Redeemer City to City, 2020).

15. Ibid.

16. Ibid.

17. The Daily Wire, "Daily Wire Backstage: Live in Long Beach," uploaded August 22, 2019, YouTube video, 1:46:43, https://www.youtube.com/watch?v=EAbuWCWv8kE.

18. Williams, "Self-Worship."

19. Ibid.

20. Ibid.

21. Dreher, *Live Not by Lies*.

22. Stafford, "Christian resistance.'"

— 15 —

The Me Generation

We've just retraced our historical steps back to Doctor Spock, who wooed the boomer generation and subsequent generations to turn away from biblically training their children. This indulgent and permissive style of parenting produced self-centred children and young adults. The departure from traditional child training also impacted the church in the West, with Christian parents unwittingly embracing Spock's permissive parenting ideas more and more. At the same time, many evangelical churches adopted new entertainment styles of worship and teaching, which focused more on getting people on seats and keeping them there. This resulted in the loss of strong structures of discipleship training. Indeed, the world has been stealthily converting the church to the cult of the self.

This chapter provides a glimpse of what we are seeing with young people today. In reality, the me generation could be any generation that is raised with indulgent and permissive parenting, but the focus here is on Gen Z. The purpose is to provide a profile of the landscape and highlight the desperate need for another Jesus revolution amongst young people. Christians need to identify and slay the monster of self and be transformed to display God's glory in purity, selflessness, and brotherly love.

Increasing Godlessness

Academic and author Phil Zuckerman, in an article in the *Los Angeles Times*, suggests that the 'increasing godlessness in America is actually a good thing'.[1] He goes on to explain how secularisation within nations lowers crime.

As much as this claim can be debated and debunked, Zuckerman does not take into consideration the rise of brokenness that we see through the rising rates of family breakup, fatherlessness, addictions, suicide, a pornography explosion, and domestic violence. Add to that skyrocketing depression and anxiety, meaninglessness, abortion, sexualisation of society, gender confusion, and more. It seems that Zuckerman, like so many from academia, is singularly focused on the destruction of religion, namely Christianity. This has blinded him to what human flourishing might look like.

JP DeGance, co-author of *End Game: The Church's Strategic Move to Save Faith and Family* explains how the 1960s' counter-culture 'decoupled' sex from marriage to where it became more or less a recreational activity.[2] Marriage was then decoupled from parenting to the point now where sex is decoupled from relationship. Our culture has 'decoupled and disconnected partnering and parenting'.[3] Through all of this, DeGance claims that the collapse of Christianity 'can be entirely explained through the drop in intact marriages … The collapse of marriage leads to a collapse of faith … Failure to attach to a dad is one of the largest psychological impediments to belief in God'. As a result of this understanding, DeGance's church focuses on supporting marriage and healthy relationships in his local area. DeGance also claims that two to six billion dollars annually is spent on youth evangelism 'yet the people that this ministry is intended to serve are the exact people that are leaving the church in droves, it's not working'.

Not only are young people disconnected; they are also incredibly wounded, and the 'woundedness of our relationships has made it impossible for people frequently to hear and receive the message of Jesus'.[4]

JP DeGance and his church make a significant difference in their community by helping families find their way back to health and wholeness through supporting marriages.

Indeed, this is just one example of how a local church conserves and strengthens the great institutions of marriage and family and, thereby, holding out a guiding light for those who need help.

The Digital Revolution

Gen Z, today's generation, are what some describe as digital natives. Born between 1995 and 2015, they can be described as follows:

> These young people have a natural language and digital environment because they have adopted technology in the first instance. Technological tools occupy a central place in their lives. They depend on them for all kinds of daily issues, from socializing or studying to shopping, getting information, having fun, etc. That is why they no longer know an era without constant connection to the world.[5]

And with this constant connection to the world, there has been no other time in history when this ubiquitous presence has the capacity to influence and direct young minds, both for good and evil. And at no other time have they been so distracted by frivolous entertainment and diversions. You only have to jump on TikTok or Instagram to be overwhelmed with young people crying out 'Look at me!' and trying to one up the next person.

Endless content streams trap viewers in a constant scroll of mindless short clips and self-comparison.

Interestingly, the internet had its very first beginnings in the '60s during the cultural revolution. Quietly in the background, two computers transmitted data for the first time, node to node. These computers were the size of a house. Little did ordinary folk anticipate the progress leading to the launch of a World Wide Web in 1993 that would enable people across the world to send files to each other and retrieve information. From there, the rapidly escalating technological advances ensured our immediate and continual connection to others around the globe. Technology brought mankind together as global citizens. All people across the world are now connected.

School children are encouraged by messages like this:

> In the emerging digital world, the international community is getting closer and closer, yet if one chooses not to act, it's easy to stay in a bubble.[6]

Our digital natives are connected to a world of unreality. They perpetually and directly connect to celebrity 'influencers', including pop artists and budding YouTubers. And this distraction disconnects them from the most important and essential connections a child needs, that is, a father and mother within a stable family. In addition, children also need a supportive, immediate community around them: a school, church, youth group, sports group, or such that provides them with stability and belonging.

One millennial I spoke to disagreed that young people are not able to experience connection online. She wrote to me:

> Many would argue that this generation does find belonging online -- particularly on social media. So often creators will refer to their followers as 'family' and

the comments are filled with threads of people pouring out their hearts, relating to whatever is being talked about and finding comfort in other strangers doing the same thing. Social media creators foster places online where their followers feel like they do finally belong somewhere. I couldn't tell you the number of times I've seen comments like "thank you so much for talking about this, I thought I was alone," or "I feel seen" – or the number of times I've come across a comment where someone has poured out their trauma, only to have people console them, send their "love", offer advice, or respond with their own. That being said, many who have found that community online are often lonely in real life – so how is online community not a supplement for it in reality?

That is a very good question, but also an indication of the demise of family and community. Technology has certainly been incredibly beneficial to the flourishing of mankind, however the potential for negative effects is just as powerful. Our digital natives want to be more connected and supported in the online metaverse than with their own flesh and blood. Sadly, this is evidence of the brokenness of our God-given institutions of fatherhood, motherhood, and family.

The Metaverse

Just when you thought you might be understanding a little about our new digital natives and the global citizen ideas, Big Tech ramps it up again. The Metaverse or Meta is a new initiative from Mark Zuckerberg where 'the digital and physical worlds converge'.[7]

> The metaverse he [Zuckerberg] imagined was a virtual environment where users (via digital avatars) could interact with each other in real time.
>
> In this vast and immersive one-stop shop, users can play games, buy digital commodities including real estate, go to school, watch the news, meet people, and so on.
>
> From one perspective, it's the next version of the internet.
>
> From another, it's just a better version of the online world Second Life, which launched in 2003 (and is still puttering along).[8]

So now we can be separate from our bodies and get out and about in a metaverse of our choosing in an avatar body—an embodiment of myself, a character that represents me online in the metaverse. This could replace my real-life social environment. I wouldn't need to take my actual body out to socialise because I could be completely unmoored from my body and alienated from physical interaction.

Watch for the impact this might have on Gen Z.

The Loneliness Epidemic

Author Jeremy Adams, of *Hollowed Out: A Warning about America's Next Generation* (2021), has been a high school teacher for twenty-five years. Along with fellow teachers, he is sounding the alarm to the world about the dramatic changes he has witnessed in students over the last five to ten years. I highly recommend his book as it provides incredible insight into the youth culture of today and the impact of technology upon our digital natives.

He observes that young people today:

> ...live largely solitary lives, inextricably connected to their phones but largely disconnected from parents, churches and communities. Instead, they eat alone, they study alone, they even socialize alone in a virtual world untethered to the physical. They are often friendless and depressed, which explains why they harm themselves and commit suicide at a rate unrivalled in American history—a history incidentally, that they see as a sordid tale of endless oppression and sprawling injustices.[9]

Adams explains how teachers recognise the drivers of modern life through their students—things like technology trends: thousands of videos, photos, comments and so on that go viral, to the background changes in parental behaviour. He states that younger kids today are digital hermits and have uniformed values. In addition, he says their curiosity is stunted, their reason is undeveloped, and their humanity is diminished.[10] They dismiss religion, are not interested in marriage and family, and are not patriotic. This has meant that they have become 'unfamiliar to the older generation'. All this is evidence of the destructive ideologies we already discussed.

According to Adams, young people are more connected digitally and yet lonelier than any other generation. They average a daily screen time of over seven hours, so human interaction is greatly reduced.[11] And with pandemic lockdowns and other government-mitigating procedures, such as school via Zoom, children and adolescent's social capacity and ability to be attentive is significantly diminished.[12] Adams quotes John Cacioppo (1951–2018), who said that loneliness isn't the lack of people, it is 'the sense you aren't sharing anything meaningful with the people around you'.[13]

Adams also refers to Professor Robert Putnam's book *Bowling Alone*, which explains that America (and the West in general) has declining rates of 'social capital'.[14] Put simply, social capital is 'the value derived from positive connections between people'.[15] Adams explains that the internet and smart phones steal our social capital. He goes on to quote that 54 percent of Americans feel lonely and 70 percent of people aged ten to forty classify themselves as lonely.[16] He also quotes another poll finding *almost one quarter of millennials could not name a single friend.*

According to Julianne Holt-Lunstad, a professor of psychology and neuroscience at Brigham Young University in Utah, USA:

> There is robust evidence that social isolation and loneliness significantly increase risk for premature mortality, and the magnitude of the risk exceeds that of many leading health indicators, ... Many nations around the world now suggest we are facing a 'loneliness epidemic.'[17]

Loneliness is most common in individuals aged over 75 and also in young people. A recent Australian study found that one in eight young people aged 16 to 25 experience very high-intensity loneliness.[18]

This information is devastating and, considering the exacerbation of extended COVID pandemic lockdowns, we may never realise the full impact of this loneliness epidemic.

Who would have imagined that the invention of the internet back in the '60s would have led to the digital natives of today and all the complexities and trappings of their digitalised lifestyle?

Untethered Orphans

Adams said this about Gen Z:

> ... they seem mysteriously barren of the behaviours, values and hopes from which human beings have traditionally found higher meaning, grand purpose or even simple contentment–and little that is worthwhile has filled this vacancy. ... Those who came before them, their parents, cultural leaders, political leaders, and yes, educators – were too often accomplices in letting these same values, virtues, traditions, and aspirations slip away, assuming that somehow their loss would be made good later or that they really didn't matter after all or that they were hindrances that should be willfully ignored. Rather than setting "high expectations" for students, we settled for "understanding" them. Unfortunately, high expectations were often not being instilled at home or in church or in other institutions either.[19]

Don't miss the point: the generations before our digital natives let our important traditions and higher values slip away. Adams observes that there is a tug-of-war between students and teachers about what it means to be human, how to find fulfilment and how to seek 'transcendent' or 'objective goods' like skills, knowledge, and wisdom.[20] But, says Adams, students are pulling on the other end of the rope because they:

> have already "won" – or, more accurately, they represent the winning side. Post-modernism is not ascendent, it is triumphant; it is how my students live and see the world; it represents their underlying assumptions, and they are no more aware of its impact on their minds and souls than a fish is cognizant of water. To young people,

> radical individualism is not emblematic of being a renegade, an iconoclast or a rulebreaker; it is not zealotry; it is, in a strange way, its own banal conformism. Yet it is revolutionary."[21]

Adams goes on to explain how the young people he teaches believe that the past 'is not only irrelevant, but wrong'. And it is not difficult to identify where these ideas originated. Young people today carry a post-modern conceit that the self does not need instructing; it needs to be validated, and it is 'not ashamed to seek satiation'.[22] This generation of young people looks within themselves to what Adams calls the 'Almighty Mirror of the frivolous self' and behold themselves to orientate themselves and find their life purpose. With no universal laws or moral codes, Adams writes that the self cannot be judged, and it demands to not be judged. Just as there is no higher goal or morals to strive for, likewise Adams contends there is no depth of depravity or immorality that one needs to make restitution for.

To stress again, this generation's untethered orphans, our digital natives, the me generation, are more anxious, more depressed, more disconnected, more distracted, and intensely lonelier than any other generation. They are in desperate need of meaningful connection and hope. They are uncritically absorbing the propaganda that purposely keeps them believing and living lies.

And this is why millennials are waking up and looking to find their way back to things of the past that were lost—the timeless, stabilising structures removed by the well-intentioned baby boomers.

Church, we must wake up, shake free from our bondage to self, prepare our hearts, fill our lamps, and ensure our light burns brightly to receive those who are searching for the solid Rock.

The next revolution surely must be amongst God's own.

1. Phil Zuckerman, "Op-Ed: Why America's record godlessness is good news for the nation," *Yahoo News*, republished from *Los Angeles Times*, April 2, 2021, https://news.yahoo.com/op-ed-why-americas-record-100647418.html.
2. The Eric Metaxas Radio Show, "JP DeGance | Endgame: The Church's Strategic Move to Save Faith and Family in America," uploaded September 28, 2021, Metaxastalk video, https://metaxastalk.com/video/jp-degance-endgame-the-churchs-strategic-move-to-save-faith-and-family-in-america/.
3. Ibid.
4. Ibid.
5. David Perry, "Digital Natives: Everything You Need to Know about the New Generation Z," R&P, April 13, 2021, https://revenuesandprofits.com/digital-natives.
6. "What Is Global Citizenship?" Global Citizen Year, accessed October 2, 2021, https://www.globalcitizenyear.org/content/global-citizenship.
7. James Purtill, "What's the metaverse and why should we care about it?" ABC Science, August 25, 2021, https://www.abc.net.au/news/science/2021-08-26/metaverse-what-is-it-why-should-we-care-about-it/100402598.
8. Ibid.
9. Jeremy S. Adams, *Hollowed Out: A Warning about America's Next Generation* (Washington, D.C.: Regnery Publishing, 2021), chapter 1.
10. Ibid.
11. Ibid.
12. Cindy Drukier, "Lower IQ, Brain Damage, Anxiety—Children Pay a High Price for Pandemic Policies," Epoch TV, The Nation Speaks, December 25, 2021, https://www.theepochtimes.com/lower-iq-brain-damage-anxiety-children-pay-high-price-for-pandemic-policies_4177325.html.
13. Adams, *Hollowed Out,* chapter 2.
14. Ibid.
15. Dr. Rick L. Mask, "What Is Social Capital and Why Is It So Important?" Southern New Hampshire University, November 19, 2019, https://www.snhu.edu/about-us/newsroom/business/what-is-social-capital.
16. Adams, chapter 2.
17. "Loneliness: A New Public Health Challenge Emerges," Vic Health, accessed 4 October, 2021, https://www.vichealth.vic.gov.au/letter/articles/vh-letter-47-loneliness.
18. Ibid.
19. Adams, chapter 1.
20. Adams, chapter 2.
21. Ibid.
22. Ibid.

— 16 —

The Early Church Counter-Culture

Young Christians today are asking the question: How can we live in the world counterculturally? Or how can we be *in* the world but not *of* the world? I believe they ask this question because the church does not adequately demonstrate how to live counterculturally as Christians. There is very little distinction in world view between those who profess Christ and those who don't.

Many biblical scholars believe that we are living in a pagan society that's not unlike that of the early church. And by studying the early church, there is much to learn. Therefore, I begin this chapter with a story recorded in *Foxe's Book of Martyrs* of a group of young Christians who were imprisoned and sent to the arena for their faith. Afterwards, I follow with some lessons we can learn from the early church.

Can I Be Called Anything but What I Am?

Carthage was a leading city in Roman Africa, now modern-day Tunisia. The Proconsul Hilarianus scheduled a public event—a day of games and spectacles performed in the city's amphitheatre—to celebrate the birthday of the emperor's son. The Roman society was hierarchical, so the people were seated according to their importance. In the arena were the victims—animals, gladiators, and criminals. During these times, criminals were allowed to be sold to use in games. This gave much more entertainment and also served as a public warning to not do what the criminals had done. It also gave a visual enforcement of the vertical society by the seating arrangements and public exhibition of the wealthy nobles and governing class.

So on the day of 7th March, AD 203, the people of Carthage went to the amphitheatre to participate in the public event, a common recreational activity. According to their normal customs, they gathered to watch their equivalent of a football match. But on this day, the people of Carthage encountered something different; they saw Christians in the ring whose behaviour challenged the values of the norm. The crowds were emotionally engaged, wavering between captivation, fury, attraction, and hate. An eyewitness account was written about this event, particularly focusing on a young lady named Perpetua, who was about twenty-one and who, unlike the others in her group who were poor and slaves, was of noble birth and educated.

The group of about six were from a small town about thirty-five miles from Carthage, and they were what was known as 'catechumens' or new converts preparing for baptism, which they received while there in prison. Their teacher Saturus was arrested and joined them; it appears he may have done this on purpose to encourage and stand with them to the end. The night before, they celebrated a last supper in front of onlookers who had come to check out the entertainment for the games.

The prisoners had a few weeks after their arrest to prepare their hearts and minds for this situation. One young woman, Felicitas, was a slave girl, and she had just given birth the day before they were to go to the arena. She was believed to be about fourteen years old. The Christians prayed that the delivery would happen so that her baby would be saved.

Perpetua's father, a nobleman, came to her in prison to try to save her. He was a pagan, and he saw an easy way for Perpetua to save herself. He entreated her simply to deny she was a Christian. In one of the many conversations, no doubt frustrating for her father, it is recorded that Perpetua said to her father:

'Father, do you see this pitcher here?' she replied. 'Could it be called by any other name than what it is?'

'No,' he replied.

'Well, neither can I be called anything other than what I am, a Christian.'[1]

When the day came, the little band marched into the arena triumphantly, without cringing. They had steeled themselves for this, even though they did not fully know what to expect. The officials demanded them to dress up as gods and priestesses. They refused, not wanting to be denied their identity. Perpetua spoke on behalf of the group that they would not wear the costumes, and the officials relented. Some accounts claim that they were forced to be naked.

The two women, Perpetua and Felicitas were charged by a wild cow that had been provoked to attack. Perpetua got up and went to help her friend Felicitas to her feet. The crowd were confused about a noble helping a slave girl. This was unfamiliar to a culture where nobility did not look out for those beneath them, particularly slaves.

Over the course of the 'games', gladiators and wild animals attacked the Christians. At the very end, the little band helped each other up, all bloodied and gored. They gathered themselves together and gave each other their last farewell kiss. With them in the ring was a prison guard—an officer converted while guarding the prisoners. Saturus, the 'father' of the little band, encouraged the guard by taking his ring, dipping it into his own blood, and giving it back to the guard saying, 'Remember me and remember the faith.'

Then they kissed each other farewell with a kiss of peace before being run through with a sword, and in doing so, they completed their martyrdom. They displayed a love for each other that transcended social barriers—brotherly love.

The crowd reacted in different ways. Most were indifferent, but some were jarred from their former ways of thinking and acting. It is reported that some became believers.

The Neopaganism of the West

Many academics purport that the West is now a pagan society or civilisation. That is, it is no longer dominated by Christian thinking, ideas, art, and philosophy. A recent book by Chantal Delsol—a French political theorist, titled *The End of the Christian World (translation from French)*, puts forth a convincing argument about the paganisation of the West. A *New York Times* article, 'Is the West Becoming Pagan Again', provides insightful commentary on her book:

> ... we are living through the end of Christian civilization — a civilization that began (roughly) with the Roman rout of pagan holdouts in the late fourth century and ended (roughly) with Pope John XXIII's [1958-1963] embrace of religious pluralism and the West's legalization of abortion ... Ms. Delsol's ingenious approach is to examine the civilizational change underway in light of that last one 1,600 years ago. Christians brought what she calls a "normative inversion" to pagan Rome. That is, they prized much that the Romans held in contempt and condemned

The Early Church Counter-Culture

> much that the Romans prized, particularly in matters related to sex and family. Today the Christian overlay on Western cultural life is being removed, revealing a lot of pagan urges that it covered up.
>
> To state Ms. Delsol's argument crudely, what is happening today is an undoing, but it is also a redoing. We are inverting the normative inversion. We are repaganizing ... Paganism never had a precise definition. The word was a catchall for those who rejected the Christian revelation, whether polytheists, nature-worshipers or agnostics. The pagus was the countryside. The Latin word "paganus," like the English word "heathen," ... [2]

During the early church era, before Constantine embraced Christianity as a state religion, Christians were actually referred to as pagans, or described as backward, for not worshipping the Roman gods.

So what was the culture of that time? Alan Kreider in his book *The Patient Ferment of the Early Church: The Improbable Rise of Christianity in the Roman Empire*, outlines some significant features that I'll summarise.[3]

First, Romans were a highly religious people, worshipping many gods that they attempted to continually appease through sacrifice and rituals. This would ensure that all would go well for them, from winning battles when their armies went to war to protecting their cities. Tim Keller expresses it well in his article 'What We Need to Learn from the Early Church':

> It was expected that people would have their own gods, but that they'd be willing to show honor to all other gods as well. Nearly every home, every city, every professional guild—including the empire itself—each had its own gods. You couldn't even go to a meal in a

large home or to a public event without being expected to do some ritual to honor the gods of that particular group or place. To not do so was highly insulting, at the least to the house or community. It was also dangerous, since it was thought that such behavior could elicit the anger of the gods. Indeed, it was seen as treason to not honor the gods of the empire, on whose divine authority its legitimacy was based.[4]

In addition to this, Romans were also highly superstitious, believing in omens and practicing augury—divination by watching natural signs such as the birds, weather, etc.

Roman culture was violent even in peacetime. The gladiatorial games were fights to the death. People were entertained by the mass killing of unarmed criminals, including Christians, or by animals killing each other and killing humans. They had a distinct love of bloodshed. The games were seen as a Roman rite, with the attendants in the arena dressed up as gods.

Romans practiced slavery. Many people owned slaves they'd acquired from conquered people groups, and the owners had complete rights to them. Slaves had no rights, yet their owners even had the right to kill their slaves.

The Romans also practiced infant exposure—the equivalent of post-birth abortion. If a baby was not wanted, it would be put on a dung hill or trash heap to die. The father of the baby had a right to decide if the baby would live or die.

Roman society was a vertical or hierarchical society. It started at the top with the emperor, who had the most power and wealth, then came those appointed to governing positions then the wealthy nobles (what we would call the elites). It worked down the chain to people of lowest value and rank in society, and these had no rights. The rich 'felt no obligation to care for them [the poor] or increase their lot in life'.[5]

Finally, women were considered inferior to men. Married women of noble birth were required to remain faithful and monogamous; however, the men were free to have sex outside the marriage, including with slaves, prostitutes, and children.

The Inversion of Christianity

Christians were an 'inversion' of the Roman culture of the first three centuries. They were 'a contrast community, a counterculture that was both offensive and yet also attractive to many'.[6]

What made the Christian community so different?

Early church scholars have provided excellent insights. Tim Keller, in his article '5 Features That Made the Early Church Unique', takes his insights from books by the late Larry Hurtado, a New Testament and early church scholar who wrote two insightful tomes, *Why on Earth Did Anyone Become a Christian in the First Three Centuries?* and *Destroyer of the gods: Early Christian Distinctiveness in the Roman World*.

And distinctiveness is the key. Keller writes:

> Hurtado points out that the basis for this unusual social project was the unique religious identity of Christians. Before Christianity, there was no distinct "religious identity," since your religion was simply an aspect of your ethnic or national identity. If you were from this city, or from this tribe, or from this nation, you worshiped the gods of that city, tribe, or people. Your religion was basically assigned to you.
>
> Christianity brought into human thought for the first time the concept that you chose your religion, regardless of your race and class. Christianity also radically asserted that your faith in Christ became your new, deepest

> identity, while at the same time not effacing or wiping out your race, class, and gender. Instead, your relationship to Christ demoted them to second place. This meant, to the shock of Roman society, that all Christians—whether slave, free, or highborn, or whatever their race and nationality—were now equal in Christ (Gal. 3:26–29). This was a radical challenge to the entrenched social structure and divisions of Roman society, and from it flowed at least five unique features.[7]

Here is a summary of Keller's points with some of my own explanations:

1. Keller discusses the unity of the early church. The biblical world view taught that all men were created equal in value before God, so they imposed no ethnic or hierarchical boundaries. The rich and poor, male and female, slave and free, Black and White were all the same in the eyes of God. Therefore, Perpetua being of noble standing and helping a slave girl was shocking and perplexing for the crowd to witness.

2. The early church was a community of forgiveness and reconciliation. The culture of the day was a shame and honour culture, and within those cultures, when one's honour was violated, retaliation and revenge were expected. Christians did not react in this way; they were taught to practice patience and that vengeance belongs to God. This was especially hard for those who were reported by their neighbours and suffered imprisonment. Those who did not go to their death at the arena practiced incredible patience in not retaliating when released.

3. The early church was renowned for practicing hospitality to the poor and suffering. In the early church world, there were many poor. In Roman society, it is believed that around 65

percent of people lived close or below subsistence level. Kreider explains that care of the poor was a fundamental commitment the Christians made at their baptism, and the practical application of charity was a powerful cause of Christian success.[8] The early church was also a strong witness in the Roman world as they nursed the sick in the plagues of the 2nd and 3rd centuries AD. The impact of Christian mercy was so strong in the 4th century that Julian proposed the distribution of wine and grain to the poor, saying, 'The impious Galileans [Christians], in addition to their own, support ours, [and] it is shameful that our poor should be wanting our aid.' [9]

4. The early church was a community committed to the sanctity of life. Abortions in ancient times were dangerous and rare. Infant exposure was practiced more commonly—they were thrown on rubbish heaps to die. This put them at risk of being taken by traders into slavery and prostitution, so Christians would scour the dumps and adopt all they found. Refusing to participate in the taking of human life in any form at all was a basic Christian commitment; it was a product of the Christian's high value of life.

5. The sexual counter-culture was one of virtue. The sexual discipline of Christians was remarkable. Many contemporaries noted that Christians were committed to sexual purity, and they admired this. Krieder quotes one of those contemporaries, who wrote that Christians 'repudiated adulterous glances, avoided second marriages, and committed themselves to lifelong continence'. One philosopher of the time wrote that he was 'deeply impressed' by the Christians' sexual behaviour. Their 'restraint in cohabitation' compelled him to take their faith seriously.[10]

On this, Keller writes:

> Christians' sexual norms were different, of course. The church forbade any sex outside of heterosexual marriage. ... It saw sex not just as an appetite but as a way to give oneself wholly to another and, in so doing, imitate and connect to the God who gave himself in Christ. It also was more egalitarian, treating all people as equal and rejecting the double standards of gender and social status. Finally, Christianity saw sexual self-control as an exercise of human freedom, a testimony that we aren't mere pawns of our desires or fate ...[11]

Kreider identifies considerably more than Keller's five distinctives of the early church.

He also highlights a distinction in how Christians conducted their businesses—with integrity. There was no cheating customers. They were willing to speak truthfully about what they sold and did not retaliate when they were treated unethically by other businessmen. They did not follow the customary practice of giving guarantees under oath. This was forbidden for Christians. They spoke plainly and honestly and charged fair prices.

Regarding relationships, it was not the usual practice of Roman men to meet or gather with women and children, as they did with Christian fellowship. Old women were particularly despised and children ignored in pagan society. Christian families were different; they purposefully taught and trained their children in godliness. Women were very active in the early church, and it is thought that women were probably the church's most effective evangelists. New believers were attracted by Christians' love for one another.

The early Christians were known for their 'manifestations of divine power'. They were faced with forces that they saw as evil—social, economic, religious, and political—and viewed their struggle as a fight against spiritual forces that prevented them from flourishing. At times, Christians were humiliated, intimidated, and crushed. Nevertheless, they believed that they could defeat these forces through prayers for exorcism and healing. Kreider writes that according to Clement of Alexandria, when Christians joined together for worship, they were 'a ragtag "army without weapons" made up of "God-fearing old men... God-beloved orphans... widows armed with gentleness... [and] men adorned with love," they asked God for the subduing of "sickness at its height... [which would be] put to flight by the laying on of hands"; also for the shattering of "the violence of demons [which is] reduced to impotence by confident commands"'.[12] The Christians became known to their contemporaries as healers and exorcists.

Finally, Christians were known for their patience that did not compel. Christians never compelled anyone. They believed that God works by means of persuasion, that he does not use violent means to obtain what he desires. 'They felt strongly that the gospel could never be compelled upon people by coercion, which would be impatience.'[13] In fact, the early church fathers believed that the growth of the church would depend on evidence and not on forcing or pressuring people to become Christians. This was reflected in the believer's everyday behaviour, which demonstrated, through time and experience, whether their beliefs were authentic or not.

Keller writes:

> It was because the early church didn't fit in with its surrounding culture, but rather challenged it in love, that Christianity eventually had such an effect on it.[14]

Christians in Secular Culture

Christians in the West are a shrinking minority because the majority are fitting in with the surrounding culture. Even though polls might indicate that Christianity in countries like America and Australia is the dominant faith, when this is unpacked, things look much different.

A 2021 study by the Cultural Research Centre of Arizona Christian University revealed that 69 percent of Americans self-identify as Christians; however, only 6 percent 'possess a biblical world view, and demonstrate a consistent understanding and application of biblical principles.'[15] The study used dozens of questions to dig down into the world view of those who self-identified as Christians. The 6 percent represents those who had something of a functioning Christian world view by adhering to the basic truths of the Bible and seeking to live accordingly.

A secular society is a society where the culture and government operate in the absence of any common religious tradition. Western nations are secular nations culturally, not adhering to any religious authority. When the authority of a given religion is removed, individuals are left with no authority, only the authority of the self.

Natasha Crain, in her book, *Faithfully Different: Regaining Biblical Clarity in a Secular Culture*, identifies self as the tie that functionally binds the worldviews of the masses.[16] They may have many different beliefs, but it comes back to one's source of authority; and with secularism, the authority is self. This contrasts with the biblical view that God, through his inspired authoritative Word, is our ultimate authority.

The Bible tells us why secularism is so appealing. By our own nature, we want to rule ourselves, to go our own way, to determine ourselves what is right and wrong, to be our own authority and our own boss. Without a biblical world view and belief that the Bible is God's authoritative word, then there is no distinction between Christians and the majority in secular culture.

Keller writes, 'If a religion isn't different from the surrounding culture—if it doesn't critique and offer an alternative to it— it dies because it's seen as unnecessary.'[17]

Persecution of Christians Today

According to Open Doors, Christianity is likely the most persecuted religion today, with over 360 million Christians suffering 'high levels of persecution and discrimination for their faith'.[18] Afghanistan replaced North Korea as the top country for Christian persecution worldwide. Open Doors records that since the Taliban takeover in August 2021, Christians face certain death if discovered.

Persecution in these nations is not unlike that of the early church, and the growth of Christianity in nations where there is persecution is similar. New converts have to consider carefully the cost of following Jesus before committing: they must be prepared to die, be imprisoned or tortured, be separated from their families, lose their job and social status, or be constantly in hiding and go 'underground'.

Why on earth would anyone in those nations want to become a Christian?

Yet in the Muslim nation of Iran, which has high levels of persecution, Christianity is booming:

> As a clandestine phenomenon, the practice of what are sometimes called Muslim Background Believers (MBBs) lacks clergy and church buildings, but instead consists of self-starting disciples and tiny house churches of four to five members each, with either hushed singing or none

at all. Its lay leadership, in striking contrast to the mullahs who rule Iran, consists mainly of women.[19]

To repeat: they have no clergy. They are self-starting disciples who meet in tiny house churches with hushed singing or none at all. This is a stark contrast to the declining church of the West. These Iranian Christians are not simply converts sitting in church each Sunday, they are disciples making disciples and we have much to learn from them (and from the persecuted church throughout the world).

Indeed, the act of denying self and choosing God is revolutionary. Daily we are forced with the decision: Are we with God or are we against him?

Choose God and resist the world.

---

1. "Perpetua: High society believer," *Christianity Today*, February 19, 2021, https://www.christianitytoday.com/history/people/martyrs/perpetua.html.
2. Christopher Caldwell, "Is the West Becoming Pagan Again?" *New York Times*, December 29, 2021, https://www.nytimes.com/2021/12/29/opinion/christianity-paganism-woke.html.
3. Alan Kreider, *The Patient Ferment of the Early Church: The Improbable Rise of Christianity in the Roman Empire* (Grand Rapids, Michigan: Baker Publishing Group, 2016).
4. Tim Keller, "What We Need to Learn from the Early Church," The Gospel Coalition, January 6, 2017, https://www.thegospelcoalition.org/article/what-we-need-to-learn-from-early-church.
5. Peri Zahnd, "Alan Kreider's 'The Patient Ferment of the Early Church' - review by Peri Zahnd," *Clarion*, July 2, 2020, https://www.clarion-journal.com/clarion_journal_of_spirit/2020/07/alan-kreiders-the-patient-ferment-of-the-early-church-review-by-peri-zahnd.html.
6. Tim Keller, "5 Features That Made the Early Church Unique," The Gospel Coalition, January 20, 2020, https://www.thegospelcoalition.org/article/5-features-early-church-unique.
7. Ibid.
8. Alan Kreider, *The Patient Ferment of the Early Church: The Improbable Rise of Christianity in the Roman Empire* (Grand Rapids, Michigan: Baker Publishing Group, 2016), 116.

9. Kenneth Berding, "How Did Early Christians Respond to Plagues?" The Good Book Blog, Biola University, March 16, 2020, https://www.biola.edu/blogs/good-book-blog/2020/how-did-early-christians-respond-to-plagues.

10. Kreider, *The Patient Ferment*.

11. Keller, "5 Features That Made the Early Church Unique."

12. Kreider, *The Patient Ferment*.

13. Zahnd, "The Patient Ferment review."

14. Keller, "5 Features."

15. Dr. George Barna, "American Worldview Inventory 2021: Release #6," Arizona Christian University Cultural Research Center (August 31, 2021), https://www.arizonachristian.edu/wp-content/uploads/2021/08/CRC_AWVI2021_Release06_Digital_01_20210831.pdf.

16. Natasha Crain, *Faithfully Different: Regaining Biblical Clarity in a Secular Culture* (Fort Washington, Pennsylvania: Harvest House Publishers, 2022).

17. Keller, "Early Church."

18. Open Doors International, https://www.opendoors.org/en-US/.

19. Daniel Pipes, "Iran's Christian Boom | Opinion," *Newsweek*, June 24, 2021, https://www.newsweek.com/irans-christian-boom-opinion-1603388.

— 17 —

Christian Resistance

In the 2019 documentary *Sheep Among the Wolves, Volume One*, a young Iranian man was asked about how he and his fellow Christians prepare for and deal with the persecution they suffer under an oppressive Muslim regime. He tells the story about how one day he asked a fellow believer, a young Christian woman, 'What if we are all together and radical Muslims break down our door, and they start raping all the girls there?' This, apparently, is a common happening. He asked further what she would think at that moment. And this ex-radical Muslim young woman, who is now a passionate and fiery follower of Christ, said,

> 'I have given up my rights. I have given up my position. I have given up everything for Jesus. I have given up my desires. I have given up even my future. And at that moment, when they come and rape me, I will close my eyes and say, "Now I offer my body as a living sacrifice for you, as it just says in Romans 12:1."'

The young man recalled that when he heard this, he was astonished how someone could just go in the secret place of their heart and find Jesus at that moment and say, 'Lord, on my knees, I offer you my body as a living sacrifice.'

And this is what God is doing amongst the believers in Iran—the underground church. He transforms them into radical 'Christians that you can't even put into words what that girl said, and how powerfully deep ... how strong, and what grace must be on her life that she could say that so strongly and so confidently'.[1]

Although this testimony gives a picture of persecution under a dictatorial, religious regime, there is much to learn, not least that one's conversion must be authentic and life-changing. Otherwise, one will not be able to stand against the prevailing hostility to Christianity.

This chapter is about preparing Christians in the West to resist—through strengthening our basic institutions of the family and church and embracing suffering as a source of strength in the face of persecution that is surely coming.

Could Persecution Happen in the West Today?

Many believers who lived through totalitarian communism in Russia and the former Soviet countries are raising alarm bells about the soft totalitarian creep on Western nations. Rod Dreher's book, *Live Not By Lies: A Manual for Christian Dissidents* is full of stories and insights into what it looked like to live counterculturally as a Christian during those decades.[2] In fact, his inspiration for writing the book was from a concerned elderly Czechoslovakian lady, who lived under communism and saw the same pattern of soft totalitarianism gradually being introduced in her new nation of America (which inevitably means a growing hostility to Christianity). Dreher encourages young Christians to look and learn from the persecuted Christians of the communist era for insight into how to prepare for and stand against the hostility to Christianity and Christian values we are seeing today. Dreyer believes that the persecution will look more like the *Brave New World* type rather than Orwell's *1984* style.

But could this really happen today? Surely we learned our historical lessons of the past and will never repeat this sort of tyranny again? But alas, we have historical amnesia. Young people today no longer learn history in the Western education system; they learn instead about gender, diversity, and race (critical theory), and to hate their Western nations and identify more as 'global citizens'. The Australian Institute of Public Affairs has been researching and monitoring the public education system for many years and sounding the alarm for a long time.

A 2021 article titled 'How the National Curriculum Abolishes Australian Citizenship' by Scott Hargreaves reads:

> The draft national curriculum for schools is seeking to teach the next generation of Australians a progressive and utopian view of global citizenship, just as the global COVID-19 shutdown and the resurgence of authoritarian nation-states have exposed the intellectual bankruptcy of that ideology.
>
> In so doing the curriculum's own designers have abrogated their much-vaunted commitment to also teach "Critical and Creative Thinking", as their globalist world-view is woven into the fabric of the curriculum, without any examination of how it might conflict with the "Realist" perspective of a world order constituted by independent nation-states.[3]

Notice the word 'ideology' because in our national curriculum, our kids have been learning empty philosophies (or ideologies) that turn their hearts away from God. Parents beware.

Regarding persecution, the pandemic mandates of segregation and restrictions has been an ominous foreshadowing of government overreach and loss of basic freedoms. C. S. Lewis wisely said, 'Of all tyrannies a tyranny sincerely exercised for the good of its victims may be the most oppressive.'[4]

Big Brother represents the ubiquitous AI of technology, with monitoring and tracking capabilities even from our iPhone. Many remember the Edward Snowden leaks exposing the massive internet and phone surveillance of the CIA way back in 2013. More recently, the innocent tracking and check-in apps for COVID monitoring in many Western countries have made some people feel more secure and others deeply concerned about privacy. This sort of monitoring looks ominously like the Chinese social credit system, which 'is a broad regulatory framework intended to report on the "trustworthiness" of individuals, corporations, and governmental entities across China'.[5] The Chinese government can monitor where a person goes, who they are with, and what they are doing, and this greatly disadvantages Christians. Trustworthiness is relative to whatever moral and ethical system the government powers approve of, which is the supremacy of the power of the state over God.

In chapter 14, I highlighted what I believe are the two dominant reasons why Christians are losing their children to the world, that is the devastating assault on the foundational institutions of traditional Western society of:

1. The family
2. The church

Dreher identifies these two institutions as anti-totalitarian resistance cells because, in his research of the persecuted church, he found that strong families and strong Christian fellowships or local churches (usually meeting in homes) are the most effective ways for Christians to resist and persevere.[6]

The Christian Family as a Resistance Cell

If we don't want to lose our children to the world, then we must strengthen the Christian family. Christian parents need to turn back to biblical truths to inform themselves on how to raise their children—not legalistically or in fear but through the transformed lives of parents and through biblical instruction. Dreher's *Manual for Christian Dissidents* explains the importance of the family for both learning how to love others and how to live in truth.[7] If Christians don't value the family as an institution to nurture and protect at all cost, then it will not stand against the prevailing ideologies of the world that seek to destroy it.

Since Marxist critical theory teaches that the traditional family is an oppressive institution, policies and laws are continually implemented to sever parental rights, and the state is claiming more and more power over our children.[8] Doctor Spock's destructive and chaotic advice that produces me-centred kids and angry young adults needs to be rejected and exposed for what it is, and every child training book that spouts the same philosophy as well. Surely after thousands of years of biblical teaching and practical living, we should not still be at a loss on how to train children to be obedient and respectful.

In addition, the attack on motherhood (and fatherhood) through feminist ideology—that convinces women that their value is in the marketplace earning money—destroys families. Marriage must be valued and accepted and the destruction of it resisted. Churches need to help families so that mothers who want to be at home with their children can do so. Christian fathers must step up and lead their families. Dreher quotes Vaclav Benda in his essay 'The Family and the Totalitarian State':

> The family cannot survive as a community if the head and center is one of its own members. The Christian statement is simple: it has to be Christ who is the true center, and in His service, the individual members of this community share in the work of their salvation. One hopes that the well-grounded family can exist even without this distinctively religious affiliation; however, the focus of service to something "beyond," whether we call it love, truth or anything else, seems essential.[9]

As to living out our personal faith, Michael Stafford gives this inspiring admonition:

> In an age that recognises no authority above the Self that can be invoked or appealed to, personal witness becomes of paramount importance. For this reason, we must not merely speak to others of human flourishing; we must show them the garden in bloom. That is, a life more joyful, deeper, richer and fulfilling, than any existence imaginable under the slate grey skies of the Cult of the Self. Because, as Karl Rahner, S.J. has observed, a faithful Christian life is not "a duty to be painfully observed," but rather a "glorious liberation... from the enslavement of mortal fear and frustrating egoism."
>
> Through our witness, we demonstrate that an alternative to McHell exists that can be seen, touched, experienced, and most importantly, lived. Thus, we become the mechanism for Ryn's "reorientation of mind and imagination" that exposes the lies and the "great illusions" of the Cult of the Self.[10]

Parents must teach their children to 'read' the world around them and understand people and events in terms of right and wrong because we live in a day when there is no objective truth.

So many parents are not able to read the world around them because they are either too distracted with self and the cares of the world to notice or they have a dangerously low level of biblical knowledge, causing a lack of spiritual discernment. Or both. We cannot afford to not be watching what is happening in the world, and that means questioning the mainstream narrative. Just because the majority believes something doesn't make it true. The souls of our children are at stake. We must be committed and resolute in guarding our families and training our children.

Dreher puts it so well when he writes:

> In the coming totalitarianism, Christians will have to regard family life in a much more focussed, serious way. The traditional Christian family is not merely a good idea—it is also a survival strategy for the faith in a time of persecution. Christians should stop taking family life for granted, instead approaching it in a more thoughtful, disciplined way. We cannot simply live as all other families live, except that we go to church on Sunday. Holding the correct theological beliefs and having the right intentions will not be enough. Christian parents must be intentionally countercultural in their approach to family dynamics. The days of living like everybody else and hoping our children will turn out for the best are over.[11]

The Local Church Fellowship as a Resistance Cell

The spiritual church is the shining bride of Christ that stands in stunning contrast against the empty philosophies prevailing in the world today. Dreher shares a quote from *The Last Man in*

Russia by Oliver Bullough. It is the words of an atheist after hearing the Word of God expounded:

> The immorality of the Soviet society, its inhumanity and corruption, its lack of moral code or credible ideals, means that Christ's teaching comes through to those who it reaches as a shining contrast. It stresses the value of the individual, of humanness, forgiveness, gentleness, love.[12]

Christ's teaching brings life, and it is so important that Christians know the Word of God and are transformed by it. Discipleship comes both through parenting and through the local body of believers known as the church. Many converts to Christianity have not been parented well and come from dysfunctional homes—yes, even Christian homes. Therefore, it is even more important that our children and new converts are discipled well.

In the book of Acts, we are given a picture of the function of a healthy, local church fellowship:

> "Therefore let all Israel be assured of this: God has made this Jesus, whom you crucified, both Lord and Messiah." When the people heard this, they were cut to the heart and said to Peter and the other apostles, "Brothers, what shall we do?" Peter replied, "Repent and be baptized, every one of you, in the name of Jesus Christ for the forgiveness of your sins. And you will receive the gift of the Holy Spirit. The promise is for you and your children and for all who are far off—for all whom the Lord our God will call." With many other words he warned them; and he pleaded with them, "Save yourselves from this corrupt generation." Those who accepted his message were baptized, and about three thousand were added to their number that day.

> They devoted themselves to the apostles' teaching and to fellowship, to the breaking of bread and to prayer. Everyone was filled with awe at the many wonders and signs performed by the apostles. All the believers were together and had everything in common. They sold property and possessions to give to anyone who had need. Every day they continued to meet together in the temple courts. They broke bread in their homes and ate together with glad and sincere hearts, praising God and enjoying the favour of all the people. And the Lord added to their number daily those who were being saved.[13]

So the local church gathered, baptised, and made disciples. They worshipped together, prayed together, and celebrated the Lord's supper together. They gave generously and shared with each other, and they displayed brotherly love. It wasn't just the shepherd of the flock doing everything, it was the entire body. And this is what believers in the underground church in Asia and the Middle East are doing today, and the church is growing.

As to the consumerism and materialism of the world that the church has absorbed, Stafford writes:

> There must also be a difference between us and the pagans when it comes to material goods, to consumerism. In our homes, even the pots and pans must be holy (Zechariah 14:21)! Christ taught us that uncleanness comes from within. Therefore, the material things we surround ourselves with can be powerful signs of an unclean, disordered soul and of misdirected desire. In a world awash in the cheap consumerism of the Cult of the Self, our possessions and the value we attach to them speak volumes ... In an age of decadence and

> waste, in the midst of a bacchanalia [revelry], we must live modestly. The cars we drive, the houses we live in, the clothes we wear: these should reflect the humility of spirit that distinguishes those living lives of radical discipleship to Christ. Obviously, this has the air of a counter-cultural endeavour to it. Fundamentally, it is not about dropping out of society but building an alternative parallel culture within the wreck and ruin of modernity. To paraphrase Isaiah 58:12, we are the repairers of the breach and the restorers of ruined homesteads.[14]

In his book, Dreher concludes with an admonition that indeed we will be faced with a time of painful testing and persecution that will greatly challenge our faith. Christians must teach themselves how the self-centredness of the world is a rival religion and how we have absorbed the world's values into our lives, which will not sustain us under persecution.

Suffering Is a Source of Great Strength

As the world and its empty philosophies keep telling us to look inward for fulfilment, Jesus, the true revolutionary, tells us:

> Whoever would save his life will lose it, but whoever loses his life for my sake will save it. For what does it profit a man if he gains the whole world and loses or forfeits himself?[15]

Resistance involves suffering, swimming upstream in the current culture, refusing to compromise Christian values, dethroning self, lifting others, putting family and others first, and seeking to live a life that honours God. This will cost. I repeat further what Aleksandr Solzhenitsyn wrote, after years of suffering in Russian gulags:

> Accepting suffering is the beginning of our liberation ... Suffering can be the source of great strength. It gives us the power to resist. It is a gift from God that invites us to change. To start a revolution against oppression. But for me, the oppressor was no longer the totalitarian communist regime. It's not even the progressive liberal state. Meeting these hidden heroes [those who suffered in the gulags] **started a revolution against the greatest totalitarian ruler of all: myself.**[16]

Indeed, self is the greatest totalitarian ruler, and Christians in the West need to start a revolution against its tyranny.

Dreher puts it so well when he describes the value of suffering:

> To recognise the value of suffering is to rediscover a core teaching of historical Christianity, and to see clearly the pilgrim path walked by every generation of Christians since the Twelve Apostles. There is nothing more important than this when building up Christian resistance to the coming totalitarianism. It is also to declare oneself a kind of savage in today's culture—even within the culture of the church. It requires standing foursquare against much of popular Christianity, which has become a shallow self-help cult whose chief aim is not cultivating discipleship but rooting out personal anxieties. But to refuse to see suffering as a means of sanctification is to surrender, in Huxley's withering phrase, to "Christianity without tears."[17]

Oh, that we don't surrender to a Christianity without tears. Bring on the next revolution to overthrow self and radically follow Jesus!

1. FAI Studios, "Sheep Among Wolves: Volume One," uploaded February 1, 2016, YouTube video, 1:05:50, https://www.youtube.com/watch?v=Ndf8RqgNVEY.
2. Dreher, *Live Not by Lies*.
3. Scott Hargreaves, "How the National Curriculum Abolishes Australian Citizenship," Institute of Public Affairs, May 28, 2021, https://ipa.org.au/curriculum/how-the-national-curriculum-abolishes-australian-citizenship.
4. C. S. Lewis and Clyde Kilby, *A Mind Awake: An Anthology of C.S. Lewis* (Fort Washington, Pennsylvania: Harvest Books, 2003), 45.
5. Drew Donnelly, "An Introduction to the China Social Credit System," New Horizons, February 3, 2022, https://nhglobalpartners.com/china-social-credit-system-explained.
6. Dreher, 129.
7. Ibid., 129.
8. Ibid., 132.
9. Ibid., 134.
10. Stafford, "Christian resistance."
11. Dreher, 149.
12. Ibid., 157.
13. Acts 2:37–47 (NIV).
14. Stafford, "Christian resistance."
15. Luke 9:24–25 (ESV).
16. Dreher, 221.
17. Ibid., 205.

— 18 —

The Next Revolution

C. S. Lewis wrote that the world we live in is enemy-occupied territory for the Christian. 'Christianity is the story of how the rightful king has landed, you might say landed in disguise, and is calling us all to take part in a great campaign of sabotage' to damage, destroy, or hinder the enemy's advance.[1] And we cannot do that without a revolution in our own hearts to overthrow self and radically follow Jesus.

> Of course, by resistance, rebellion, and revolution, we do not mean acts of violence, nor should we conceive of them in political terms. Instead, we should look to the life of Jesus and the early Christian communities: their focus was on making the reign of God a reality in the world, not on overthrowing the existing political order. The violent political rebels, the ones who wanted to make the state the vehicle for enforcing God's will, were the Zealots. Their cause failed, and brought ruin down on Israel.[2]

Yes, the next revolution surely must be amongst God's people—to capture and cast out the hollow philosophies of the world that destroy our families and steal our children, and to stop serving our hedonistic self. We need to return to God's truth and reclaim our identity as blood-bought children of God. And we need to disciple our kids and new converts or else they will not stand against the prevailing pressure to conform to the world.

The gospel message first went to Jesus's own people, but it was too revolutionary for the religious leaders to accept. Those who did became the counter-culture. They, in turn, took the message out to the pagan Roman world, and those who received the message lived counterculturally and did not bow down to the pagan gods, many paying for it with their lives, as we have seen.

Jesus Chose Twelve Young Men

The Mark Drama is a visual presentation of the life of Jesus according to the gospel of Mark. Viewing the performance, I was struck by the way the disciples were portrayed. They watched Jesus interact with crowds and individuals with youthful enthusiasm and wonderment. They were with him when he performed some of the strangest miracles, when he was moved by compassion, when he was indignant, when he wept, when he was provoked by his enemies, and when he calmed the storm.

According to Jewish tradition, a young man usually starts to follow a rabbi before he turns twenty.[3] It's believed that most of Jesus's disciples were teenagers. Jesus started his ministry at thirty, and he referred to his disciples as 'little children'. Peter was the only one recorded as married.

The disciples argued about things like who was the greatest, and what Jesus meant when he warned them to beware the yeast of the Pharisees; did he mean that they hadn't brought enough bread? They rebuked Jesus for saying that he was to be killed. The disciples even wanted to call down fire from heaven to destroy people. So often, they just didn't get what Jesus was talking about.

They picked corn on the Sabbath; they went out in twos on journeys and took nothing; they shook the dust off their feet. Some of them tried, unsuccessfully, to cast a demon out of a boy while Jesus was on the mountain being transfigured. One of them tried to walk on water. They were surprised to see their teacher speak to an unclean Samaritan woman or sleep at inappropriate times or touch lepers or turn tables in the temple. The teachers of the Law found so many things wrong with Jesus and his young disciples' theology and practice because it lay outside their traditional ways.

Jesus was a radical and so were his followers. At one point, the disciples told someone who was casting out demons in Jesus's name to stop. Jesus said, 'Do not stop him, ... For no one who does a miracle in my name can in the next moment say anything bad about me, for whoever is not against us is for us' (Mark 9:39–40 NIV).

Anyone who trains enthusiastic young people, including parents and teachers, knows that they make lots of mistakes. This is no different as they learn to follow Christ. And, unfortunately, in this high-tech era, those mistakes are often made public.

Imagine being at the arrest of Jesus in Gethsemane and later seeing a video taken by a bystander on their phone. CNN gets hold of the amateur video and posts it with this headline: 'Youth Flees Naked after Companion Hacks off Officer's Ear' or 'Young Man Plucked from the Sea after Attempting to Walk on Water' or 'Jewish Rabbi Touches Lepers without Mask and Gloves'. How about stories from Acts? 'Christians Found Crowding in Small Spaces to Pray' or 'Incarcerated Young Men Refuse to Stop Singing: Prison Health Officials Worried'.

Young people are radical. Those disciples were not just a bunch of crazy kids; they went out into the world and made disciples and taught those disciples, who made more disciples, who made

The Next Revolution

more disciples. They suffered beatings, persecution, imprisonment, and death, but it didn't stop them.

In fact, the following account of Moravian missionaries highlights the distinct and radical love that true believers have for their Saviour:

> Two young Moravians heard of an island in the West Indies where an atheist British owner had 2000 to 3000 slaves. And the owner had said, "No preacher, no clergyman, will ever stay on this island. If he's shipwrecked we'll keep him in a separate house until he has to leave, but he's never going to talk to any of us about God, I'm through with all that nonsense." Three thousand slaves from the jungles of Africa brought to an island in the Atlantic and there to live and die without hearing of Christ.
>
> Several thousand black slaves toiled in the sugar cane fields under the burning sun. 3000 slaves were doomed to live and die without hearing of Christ.
>
> Two young Germans in their 20's from the Moravians sect heard about their plight. They [were willing to sell themselves] to the British planter for the standard price for a male slave [if necessary.]
>
> The Moravian community from Herrenhut [sic] came to see the two lads off, who would never return again, having freely sold themselves into a lifetime of slavery. As a member of the slave community they would witness as Christians to the love of God.
>
> Family members were emotional, weeping. Was their extreme sacrifice wise? Was it necessary? The housings had been cast off and were curled up on the pier. As the ship slipped away with the tide and the gap widened,

the young men linked arms, raised their hands and shouted across the spreading gap, "May the Lamb that was slain receive the reward of His suffering."

This became the call of Moravian missions. And this is our only reason for being ... **that the Lamb that was slain may receive the reward of His suffering!** Amen.[4]

Their decisions impacted the world. This is so opposite to the platforming of today's celebrity Christians, posting their 'selfless' good deeds on social media before their 'followers'.

Our Saviour, Christ Jesus, modelled discipleship; he intensively trained young men for three years. Discipleship doesn't happen in an hour-long session, it doesn't happen going to church once a week, it doesn't happen at Sunday school or youth group. Discipleship happens in small groups, first in the family and then in small group meetings. It's purposeful. It's regular.

The two young Moravians were taught well, so well that they fully understood the gospel and the sacrifice of the blood of the Lamb. With a powerful testimony of salvation and deliverance, they loved not their lives unto the death.

It Started with Prayer

These young Moravians were the fruit of an incredible prayer movement that lasted 110 years, and it was led by Count Zinzendorf, who was only twenty-seven at the time it began. After an all-night prayer meeting in August 1727, his group decided to start a prayer vigil in their little village community of Hernnhut, Germany. They divided the week into 128 one-hour time slots and allocated people to pray. The slots were filled by two to three people per hour. Twenty-four hours a day, seven days per week, little groups met at the place of prayer, and this went on for 110 years. As they prayed, it is recorded that their hearts began to burn with the things that were on the heart of God, and one was the unreached peoples of the world. Even though their group numbered only three hundred, they sent out seventy missionaries to unreached people groups across the world over a fifteen-year time frame.[5] That's nearly 25 percent of their prayer group that gave up all to go to the farthest ends of the earth.

> Was there ever in the whole of church history such an astonishing prayer meeting as that which beginning in 1727 went on one hundred years … The best antidote for a powerless Church is the influence of a praying man.[6]

Count Zinzendorf developed a passion for prayer in his youth. In fact, when he completed college at sixteen years of age, 'he handed the famous professor Franke a list of seven praying societies'.[7]

The history of all revivals and awakenings started with prayer. One can read scores of accounts of Christians who committed themselves to meet for the kind of regular prayer that sparked an outpouring of God's Spirit and revival—accounts like those relating to the 1859 revival, when one man started a prayer meeting two years before in an upper room of a Dutch Reform building in Manhattan. Six people turned up. The next week there were fourteen, then twenty-three. Then it was decided to meet daily, and other churches in the city joined. Prayer meetings spread across the city and beyond.

> Horace Greeley, the famous editor, sent a reporter with horse and buggy racing around the prayer meetings to see how many men were praying: in one hour, he could get to only twelve meetings, but he counted 6100 men attending. Then a landslide of prayer began, which overflowed to the churches in the evenings. People

began to be converted, ten thousand a week in New York City alone.[8]

Or on a smaller scale, the account of a missionary school in Ootacamund in South India, where out of 130 boys, 100 were converted at a meeting missionary R. T. Naish visited.

> ... with almost all of these there was deep conviction of sin and much brokenness. It took the staff completely by surprise, for they had no expectation of it and were unable to cope with it. One day the lads were ordinary boys, full of fun, mischief and distraction. The next they were singing hymns all day, became intensely Bible-conscious, many spontaneously desired baptism and the communion table was filled with devoted converts.
>
> What was the explanation for this sudden movement? It was afterwards discovered that three boys, under the age of twelve had been going out in the early morning to the edge of the jungle to pray. They had prevailed with God and He had answered by fire.[9]

This was the effect of just three boys under the age of twelve. God answered their prayers.

What if Christians across our nation began to meet daily in small prayer groups, homes, parks, churches, cafes, or even somewhere like the edge of the jungle to pray for the lost, the broken, and those sitting in darkness? What if?

A prayer hub movement has already begun in the West with small groups meeting together for prayer, out of sight of social media, publicity, and the platforming of Christian 'celebrities'. It is counter-cultural and Spirit driven.

I Want God and I Want Freedom

And finally, back to John the Savage from *Brave New World*, the modern, technical world with every comfort available. Back to our secular, humanistic, hedonistic, and self-centred culture that pursues pleasure and happiness and avoids pain at all cost. John appeals to the head of the World State (Mustapha Mond) to return to the wilds of the woods rather than remain in the comforts of civilisation and the soma-induced mindlessness of that life. Mustapha tries to convince him to stay in the World State:

> And if ever, by some unlucky chance, anything unpleasant should somehow happen, why, there's always soma to give you a holiday from the facts. And there's always soma to calm your anger, to reconcile you to your enemies, to make you patient and long-suffering. In the past you could only accomplish these things by making a great effort and after years of hard moral training. Now, you swallow two or three half gramme tablets, and there you are. Anybody can be virtuous now. You can carry at least half your morality about in a bottle. Christianity without tears–that's what soma is.[10]

John the Savage, who represents the yearnings of many millennials, answers with such beautiful conviction and full awareness of what he is asking for:

> 'But I don't want comfort. I want God, I want poetry, I want real danger, I want freedom, I want goodness, I want sin.'

> 'In fact,' said Mustapha Mond, 'you're claiming the right to be unhappy.'

> 'All right then,' said the Savage defiantly, 'I'm claiming the right to be unhappy.'[11]

John the Savage chose the freedom to suffer, which was the way of real life.

As C. S. Lewis said so well, 'We have had enough, once and for all, of Hedonism—the gloomy philosophy which says that Pleasure is the only good.'[12] Yes, the hedonism of the world that has converted the church to the cult of the self.

The next revolution for Christians is to forsake the pleasures and lies of the empty philosophies of the World State and return to the old traditions of the Savage Reservation, where there is true freedom.

God offers us freedom through struggle, danger, and death; therefore, crucify self, hack it to pieces, bury it, spit on its grave, and radically follow Jesus.

Behold, I stand at the door and knock …

---

1. C. S. Lewis, *Mere Christianity* (London: Geoffrey Bles, 1952).
2. Stafford, "Christian resistance."
3. "How old were the disciples of Jesus when they joined him?" Bible Q, November 5, 2011, http://bibleq.net/answer/4801.
4. "May the lamb that was slain receive the reward of his sufferings," the Berean Call, 2014, https://www.thebereancall.org/content/may-lamb-was-slain-receive-reward-his-sufferings.
5. Martin Kim, "The Moravian 100 Year Prayer Movement!" Revivalandreformation.org, accessed May 6, 2022, https://revivalandreformation.org/resources/all/the-moravian-100-year-prayer-movement.
6. David Smithers, "Count Zinzendorf & The Moravians: Prayer Makes History," the Traveling Team, accessed May 6, 2022, http://www.thetravelingteam.org/articles/count-zinzendorf-the-moravians-prayer-makes-history.
7. Ibid.

8. J. E. Orr, "Prayer and Revival," Revival Library, accessed May 6, 2022, https://www.revival-library.org/resources/revival_speakers/revival_anecdotes/prayer_and_revival.shtml.

9. Arthur Wallis, "Prayer and Revival," Revival Library, accessed May 6, 2022, https://www.revival-library.org/resources/revival_speakers/revival_anecdotes/prayer_and_revival.shtml.

10. Aldous Huxley, *Brave New World* (New York City: Vintage, 2007), chapter

11. Ibid., chapter

12. C. S. Lewis, *Present Concerns,* Reprint edition (San Francisco: HarperOne, 2017).

ACKNOWLEDGEMENTS

Rod – my love and lifelong companion, I could not have written another book without your steadfast support and encouragement.

Adin & Lucy, Josiah & Hayley, Kezia and Elijah, Eli and Tess – my fan club who encourage me constantly and have taught me so much. I remain always your mama bear.

My YFC family – your passion for the lost is inspiring and challenging. It is my hope that you will be truly blessed by this book.

Those who read the manuscript and endured through multiple edits – I offer my sincere gratitude.

Dianne and Mike – for honest feedback, too many edits to count, and much encouragement, I'm truly thankful for you!

Danni and my prayer team – thank you so much for uplifting me in prayer throughout this writing process!

To those who contributed directly or indirectly – my deepest gratitude, including Jordan and Elisa.

My heavenly Father – your love is better than life itself, it continually sustains me.

'Give thanks to the Lord, for he is good, his mercy endures forever' (Psalm 118:29 NAB).

ABOUT THE AUTHOR

Cindy McGarvie serves as the national director of Youth for Christ Australia.

Always one for adventure, Cindy began her career by training as a nurse in the Australian Army, specialising in the operating theatre. After she left the army, she started a family with her husband, Rod, whom she met in the Australian Defence Force.

After travelling the world with their young family, Cindy and Rod felt a calling to the mission field and both trained as Bible translators with Wycliffe Australia. In 1998, they moved to East Africa and served in a leadership capacity in Uganda for eight years and then in Tanzania for four years.

During these years, Cindy discovered an interest and passion for teaching within cultural contexts. An avid reader with an insatiable curiosity, she began reading prolifically. She took external university courses in history, anthropology, and development.

Upon returning to Australia in 2010, Cindy took on the role of missions director of a large church in Brisbane for a number of years before stepping into the government sector. This fuelled her passion further for culture, politics, and social change. With a desire to serve in Christian ministry again, Cindy was appointed the national director of Youth for Christ Australia in 2015. Missions has always been her strongest passion.

Cindy serves on the board of directors of the Australian Institute of Family Counselling (AIFC) and Wycliffe Australia.

She lives with her husband, Rod, on their rural property in Northern Rivers, NSW. They have five adult children, three sons and two daughters, and three inspiring and energetic young in-laws.

www.ingramcontent.com/pod-product-compliance
Lightning Source LLC
Chambersburg PA
CBHW050307010526
44107CB00055B/2134